GAELIC GAMES

Published in 1998 by Mercier Press
PO Box 5 5 French Church Street Cork
Tel: (021) 275040; Fax: (021) 274969
e.mail: books@mercier.ie
16 Hume Street Dublin 2
Tel: (01) 661 5299; Fax: (01) 661 8583
e.mail: books@marino.ie

Trade enquiries to CMD Distribution
55A Spruce Avenue
Stillorgan Industrial Park
Blackrock County Dublin
Tel: (01) 294 2556; Fax: (01) 294 2564

© Paul Healy 1998
ISBN 1 85635 215 3
10 9 8 7 6 5 4 3 2 1
A CIP record for this title is available
from the British Library

Cover photo by Inpho
Cover design by
Penhouse Design Group
Printed in Ireland by ColourBooks
Baldoyle Industrial Estate, Dublin 13

Published in the US and Canada by
the Irish American Book Company,
6309 Monarch Park Place, Niwot,
Colorado, 80503
Tel: (303) 530-1352, (800) 452-7115
Fax: (303) 530-4488, (800) 401-9705

GAELIC GAMES

and the Gaelic Athletic Association

PAUL HEALY

MERCIER PRESS

IRISH AMERICAN BOOK COMPANY (IABC)
Boulder, Colorado

For our daughter Emma

CONTENTS

ACKNOWLEDGEMENTS

A number of people assisted me with this undertaking. The book involved a lot of research and regular consultation with 'GAA people', as I sought clarification on issues, second opinions and, of course, facts. The following assisted in these regards and also read draft chapters: Michael Naughton, Tommy Kenoy, Tommy Mullaney and John O'Callaghan. Their kind assistance is much appreciated. My thanks also to Seamus Duke, who was most helpful.

As in the past, Siobhan Brady at GAA headquarters in Croke Park was very cooperative. I wish also to express my appreciation to Sile Wallace and Helen O'Rourke for information regarding camogie and ladies' football respectively. Thanks too to Eamonn Bolger and to my colleague Noel Fallon, to my brother Liam for his assistance, and to the unwitting GAA fans whose brains I picked and views I elicited in conversation over recent months.

A special thanks to my wife Fiona for her help and support over the months during which this book was researched and written. Thanks also to Jo O'Donoghue and her colleagues at Mercier Press/Marino Books for much-appreciated encouragement, advice and guidance.

Finally, a sincere thanks to all the other people who helped in any way. Your support is much appreciated.

FOREWORD

We all know the Irish love a song and a dance. We are similarly passionate about our native games. We invest our music, sport, poetry and storytelling with imagination, wit, energy and optimism. They are expressions of what we are.

It has always been so. Over the centuries the Irish people, irrespective of how downtrodden or oppressed they might have been, cherished song and dance; the same energy and sense of fun were channelled into football and hurling, the distinctive Irish games passed from generation to generation. These were versions of the games we know today as Gaelic football and hurling. Irish football involved players and a ball, as in soccer or rugby; hurling, also known in the early days as hurley, was unique in that the participants struck a much smaller ball with a large stick, or hurley. Players and spectators enjoyed competitive encounters in the open countryside as special occasions for pleasure, an escape from life's harsh realities.

The popularity of football and hurling waxed and waned at different times in different areas; the periodic lulls were morethe result of political turmoil or economic hardship than of apathy. Over the centuries the Irish and their games remained bonded, if precariously at times. However, towards the end of the nineteenth century some people feared that the Irish games could face extinction, that English games would take over in Ireland and that the native games would fade away. The impetus to found the Gaelic Athletic Association (GAA) was part of a more general cultural revival in Ireland, most notably evident in the establishment of the Gaelic League by Douglas Hyde in 1893.

The establishment of the GAA in 1884 was the defining

moment in the history of Ireland's native games. The action taken that day by Clare schoolteacher Michael Cusack and his colleagues would ensure the revival and further development of Ireland's unique sports.

Today, the GAA regulates four distinctive games, or codes, as they are sometimes known. The most popular are Gaelic football and hurling; the others are camogie and handball. Camogie is a field game played by ladies while handball is like squash without the rackets and is played by individuals or teams of two.

GAA games are currently enjoyed by millions of people – players and spectators – every year. The state of health of the organisation and the level of support for the games are a stunning endorsement of the vision of its founders. The Association has a magnificent national stadium in Dublin, Croke Park, named after its first patron, Archbishop Croke. The GAA showpieces, the All-Ireland football and hurling finals, are held there each year.

The GAA has remained nationalistic in outlook, and for many years its members were banned from taking part in 'foreign' games, particularly the English games of soccer and rugby. This controversial ban was lifted in 1971 but to this day the GAA will not allow the playing of soccer at Croke Park and members of the British security forces based in Northern Ireland are banned from taking part in its games.

Controversial, complex, unique, inspiring, remarkable... the GAA is different things to different people. It has brought joy to millions, instilling pride and a sense of belonging. It has angered some people; it continues to intrigue. Although views on the Association may vary nobody can dispute that it is a sporting giant, an Irish institution, a phenomenon that has played a dominant role in Irish life for over a century. Now, as the new millennium approaches, the GAA looks certain to retain its hold on Ireland and the Irish.

1

THE ORIGINS

Like soccer and rugby, the games that the founders of the GAA were so anxious to see survive had their origins many centuries ago. Ball games were played in biblical times, in pre-Christian Greece and in pagan Egypt, while the early Europeans played versions of games that are now seen as forerunners to Gaelic football, hurling, soccer and rugby.

Of the distinctive Irish games, hurling's origins are furthest back in time. The Irish were wielding their hurley sticks, seemingly with dangerous abandon, thousands of years ago. Irish legend claims that in the year 2000 BC the game was being played here, and there are stories of fierce hurling battles which frequently resulted in players being killed by vicious strikes of the hurley.

Indeed the Brehon Laws, Ireland's first legal system, provided for compensation in instances where people died as a result of hurling. It was not just humans who were at risk. The Irish hero Cú Chulainn ('the hound of Culann') got his name when he hit his hurling ball (*sliotar*) at lightning speed down the throat of the fierce watchdog of Culann, killing the animal and getting himself a new job as replacement watchdog.

Violent hurling could have its advantages. King Labhraidh

Loinsech was born dumb. One day he received a fierce blow of a hurley to the shin. The pain was so great that he instantly acquired the gift of speech and presumably never stopped talking about his good fortune thereafter. Centuries ago there was a tradition that whoever scored the first goal in a game should give three kisses 'to whatever woman on the plain he wished, except only the king's wife and daughter'. The tradition has died – sadly – and it is team-mates who are now in gravest danger of being kissed when a player scores.

In later centuries the ancient game of hurling was played across fields and sometimes across the entire countryside linking two villages, with the participants aiming to strike the ball, past friend and foe, back into their own village. Each 'team' consisted of most of the village people, sometimes hundreds in number. Many were equipped with their own curved sticks; others just joined in for the fun. Along the way everyone was fair game to receive a few 'clatters' of the hurley stick. This village-to-village hurling was sometimes referred to as 'hurling to the country'. In later years the game would become more refined as the Irish developed unique skills with the hurley stick.

Gaelic football evolved in a similar manner to hurling. There are historical references to a form of Irish or Gaelic football being played in Ireland as far back as the fourteenth century. Like hurling, football games were cross-country marathons involving hundreds of 'players'. Violent exchanges were the norm. This cross-country football was called '*caid*' in County Kerry (sometimes spelt '*cad*'), taking its name from the ball of horsehide or oxhide which had an inflated natural bladder inside it.

As recently as the mid-1800s a typical game of football in Ireland involved hundreds of people playing across miles of open countryside, with the obligatory frequent pauses for bouts of wrestling and fist-fighting. The object of the game seems to have been to spend the day crossing fields while eluding flying fists and sprawling legs. The ball was more of an accessory. The game was a social event as much as a sporting one, and those who were wearing caps probably had the decency to tip them as they came upon wrestling neighbours every now and again.

'Hurling to the country' had a brief existence in England, possibly adopted by locals who had seen hurling in Ireland or had been inspired by the Scottish version of the game, shinty. The writer Richard Carew saw the game in Devon and Cornwall towards the end of the sixteenth century, and his vivid account offers us an insight into what cross-country football and hurling events were like in Ireland over the centuries.

I quote part of Carew's detailed report from Joe Lennon's book, *The Playing Rules of Football and Hurling*. Here Carew is describing the amazing attempts to get the ball from one village to the other:

> Whosoever grabs the ball, finds himself generally pursued by the adverse party; neither will they leave till (without all respects) he has been laid flat on Gods deare earth: which fall once received, disableth him from any longer detaining the ball . . . he therefore throws the ball . . . the hurlers take their next way over hilles, dales, hedges, ditches; yea and through bushes, briars, mires, plashes and rivers whatsoever; so you shall sometimes see twenty or thirty lie tugging together in the water, scrambling and scratching for the ball . . . again other troups lie hovering on

the sides, like wings to help or stop their escape
and where the ball itself goes, it resembles the
joining of the two main battles . . . yes, there are
horsemen placed also on either party (as if it were
an ambush) and ready to ride away with the
ball . . . but they must not so steal the palme: for
gallop any one of them never so fast yet he shall
be surely met at some hedge-corner, cross-lane,
bridge or deep water, which . . . they know he
must needs pass by; and if his good fortune guard
him not the better, he is likely to pay the price
of his theft with his own and his horse being
overthrown to the ground. Sometimes the whole
company runneth with the ball, seven or eight
miles out of the direct way (to the opposing goals)
which they should keep.

At the end of the 'game' they all joined up in the house of
the winning gentleman (a leading figure in the village who
organised the fun), and had a drink of beer, which is hardly
surprising after a day like that. Just as well they didn't then
have to sit down and watch highlights, analysis and slow
motion replays.

Historically, aggression has always been a feature of
Gaelic football. An eighteenth-century historical reference to
the football of the time notes that the players showed skill
at 'shouldering and tripping', while another confirms that
'wrestling was permitted'. A more gruesome picture of Irish
football was painted by a seventeenth-century report of a
game in which Irish students allegedly used a human head
as a ball. The same story crops up in Kerry folklore as an
example of man's resourcefulness in the absence of a
standard ball!

Even when football graduated to a point where two teams consisting of the same number of players met on a marked pitch, wrestling was still permitted. The attitude to this practice would be considered bizarre today. If two players started to wrestle, the remaining players were obliged to 'watch the ball' while the wrestlers indulged in battle. One fall was permitted, but if a player grounded his opponent twice, then, and only then, did the referee intervene.

Indeed if modern-day referees feel they have problems, they should perhaps think again. At times in the past, when cross-country football was the norm, referees would ride through the mayhem on horseback, as this was the safest way to do their job. Even then, some would only intervene if lives were thought to be at risk. On the credit side, referees got whistles for the first time in 1888 (after the GAA had been formed) – but on the debit side, they lost their horses somewhere along the way.

With violence rampant and organisation virtually non-existent as recently as one hundred and fifty years ago, all that could be said for Ireland's native games was that they were being handed on from generation to generation – surviving, despite their coarseness, because they offered the people brief prospects of happiness, and a respite from everyday problems.

A feature of Ireland's history was the demise and rebirth of the games at varying intervals in different counties. Their survival came under particular threat with the Great Irish Famine, which began to take its grim toll around 1847. The survival of the people became a more immediate concern than the survival of the people's games. An estimated two million of those people died and a further two million or so emigrated as a result of the hardship visited by the famine.

Within a decade or so of the catastrophe, however, a

resilient people had again turned to football and hurling as pastimes. By the early 1860s they were being played fairly extensively once more. While some attempt was made to restrict numbers involved in games, violence remained a feature and the organisation of the games still lacked direction.

MICHAEL CUSACK AND THE POLITICS OF THE 1880S

Native games were clearly in desperate need of a guiding hand, not to mention round-the-clock medical services, by the time Michael Cusack was born. Cusack was a colourful and controversial individual. An all-round sportsman, he was a champion weight-thrower and a keen hurler and footballer, having fallen in love with those games when, as a child, he first saw them played in his native Clare. When he moved to Dublin to teach, he remained actively involved in sport, while also developing a passion for politics, the Irish language and everything nationalist. Cusack realised that athletics, Gaelic football and hurling needed a governing body to help them survive.

The pending establishment of the GAA must also be seen in a political light. The Irish people were under British rule, and, as ever, many were not happy with this state of affairs. The establishment of the GAA took place at a time when the desire to gain national independence was intense, and when the influence of British games in Ireland, at the expense of the native games, was resented. The British had long dismissed the native Irish games while seeking to impose their own, or at least to have sport in Ireland subjected to British rules.

Michael Cusack and others were conscious that if British games took over in Ireland, Irish games would, in time, fade away. This view was shared by staunch nationalists who were appalled at any notion of British influence in Ireland. The question therefore is valid: was the GAA effectively started by anti-British militants?

The 1880s was a politically turbulent time. The people wanted an improvement in their economic circumstances as well as their political freedom. The Irish Republican Brotherhood (the IRB, also known as the Fenians), founded in 1858, was intent on fighting the British in a bid to gain Irish independence, and would have shared Cusack's concern about the rise of British games in Ireland. Cusack himself had been a Fenian, and the IRB – covertly – saw him as the man most capable of starting a new national association that would promote Irish games.

Meanwhile Michael Davitt, a Fenian who had been released from prison, set up the Land League (aimed at enabling Irish tenants, then at the mercy of landlords, to gain control of their land) in Mayo. Subsequently the National Land League was established.

The Land League became an immensely popular movement, and its rise coincided with a split in the Irish Republican Brotherhood. However, the Fenians continued to meet in secret. At every opportunity they supported the promotion of athletics, allegedly to keep the menfolk in peak condition for a possible rising.

The IRB then decided to set up a sub-committee which would look into the possibility of establishing an athletic movement. They duly contacted Michael Cusack, who agreed to become involved. Cusack met with Davitt, the Land League leader, to enlist his support. Davitt was all in favour of such an organisation being established. Nationalist Ireland was essentially at one: Irish games were to be revived and British influences resisted.

Michael Cusack first helped revitalise athletics, organising his own 'Cusack's Academy Sports' in Dublin's Phoenix Park.

Michael Cusack

His passion for the team games he had always loved remained, however, and he soon became instrumental in the bid to re-establish the national game of hurling, largely but not totally dormant at the time. A version of the game, 'hurley' (now hockey), was being played in some parts of the country, but it was not to Cusack's liking, being too dissimilar to the more robust game of hurling he had seen and played in his native Clare years before.

Cusack firstly set up the Dublin Hurling Club, but this venture collapsed following a row between hurley and hurling players (which they tried to resolve by clobbering each other with their hurleys). He then set up the Metropolitan Hurling Club and with some pleasure helped to orchestrate the revival of hurling at the expense of hurley.

When the Killimor Club in Galway (a county in which hurling had survived through the ages) approached the Metropolitan Club for a game, Cusack saw his chance to spread hurling and football on an organised basis. The time to act had arrived.

The GAA is Born

After a handful of failed attempts, the Clareman finally got a group of his peers to attend a meeting in Miss Hayes's Commercial Hotel in Thurles, County Tipperary. The date was 1 November 1884. Reports vary on the size of the attendance, the consensus being that between seven and thirteen men were present.

After they had exchanged pleasantries, the group took their seats in the hotel's billiards room, presumably unaware that they were about to change the course of Irish life forever. While Maurice Davin, a Tipperary man who would be the Association's first President, chaired the meeting, it was Cusack who did most of the talking. By the end of the meeting the Gaelic Athletic Association (Cumann Luthchleas Gael) had been founded. The stated aims of the strictly amateur body were to preserve and cultivate Ireland's national pastimes. Finally, Gaelic games would have a sense of direction.

Ironically, given what has evolved since, athletics were much more popular in the early days of the Association than football or hurling. While the latter games were being played in various counties at the time, athletics meetings were drawing much greater crowds. It was athletics that brought all shades of society together, with the richest man in the neigbourhood rubbing shoulders, however disapprovingly at times, with the poorest.

The first committee of the newly formed Association therefore concentrated largely on athletics meetings; it was the pragmatic thing to do. At many of these meetings hurling and football games were played as side attractions. They were second on the bill, but at least they were more structured than before, with the size of teams restricted and violent play frowned upon in those relatively enlightened times.

Soon the GAA began to try to enhance the appeal of their ball games. At their second meeting instructions were issued to have rules drawn up for these games. In early 1885 the first hurling game under GAA rules was played in Tynagh, County Galway, with 6,000 spectators turning up. A few weeks later, in February, the first football game under GAA rules was played between two local teams in Callan, County Kilkenny.

At its 1886 convention, the Association's second, it was decided that football, hurling and handball would in future be given equal prominence to athletics. At the same convention improved and more concise playing rules for football and hurling were established. In time the GAA would cease to control athletics, concentrating on ball games.

'LIKE A PRAIRIE FIRE'

Once the GAA began to turn its attention to hurling and football and to organise games independently of athletics meetings, the good times began. Virtually every household responded to the new Association. The new sense of organisation appealed to the people. Every weekend, men and women travelled by whatever means were available – usually their own feet – to play in or attend a game. The Association was taking shape rapidly. It was largely working-class in its composition, and while its appeal was widespread, it was strongest in rural areas. In addition to being seen as a nationalist organisation, the new Association was viewed as having very strong links with the Catholic Church, which had enthusiastically supported its founding. Priests played an important role in encouraging the youth of the country to respond to the Association.

Suddenly a unique parish network was woven. New hurling and football clubs were formed in every part of the country, for if one parish had a team, its neighbouring parishes invariably set one up too. The people were building foundations that have not weakened but in fact grown stronger, in the course of over one hundred years.

The first inter-county competitions, where county teams would play each other, were held in Thurles and Athlone on Easter Sunday 1886. Thousands attended. These inter-county competitions were forerunners to the provincial and All-Ireland championships we know today.

Meanwhile, in a dramatic off-field development, Michael Cusack was about to suffer the embarrassment of being removed as Secretary of the Association whose founding he had inspired. His behaviour in the position had been deemed unacceptable by his colleagues, not all of whom were well disposed towards him. Cusack had a gruff, dictatorial manner, frequently fought with his fellow officers, and was never far from controversy. It is quite understandable, of course, that his ego should have grown a little in those first years, when, in his own memorable words, the GAA spread 'like a prairie fire'.

If his ego had indeed expanded, it was abruptly deflated on 4 July 1886, when the colourful father-figure of the GAA was democratically removed as its Secretary by his peers. More reasonable men would follow in his footsteps, such as Meathman Dick Blake, who would make an outstanding contribution to the GAA as Secretary. With improved organisation, spearheaded by Blake, standards soon improved in hurling and football, with players adopting a more scientific approach to the game, and placing less of an emphasis on the use of muscle.

Off the field of play, however, the Association was

encountering many problems, which ensured that it could not rest on its laurels. Immersed in political turmoil, the GAA was vulnerable to splits, attempted takeovers, accusations of political interference and often spectacular internal squabbling.

The greatest threat to the very existence of the fledgling Association came in 1891 with the famous Parnell split. Charles Stewart Parnell led the Irish Home Rule Party in a forceful manner, but in late 1890 the party membership moved to oust him. His hold on the party had been on the wane for a short period; there were rumours that he was in poor health, while his long-standing relationship with a married woman, Kitty O'Shea, threatened to embroil him in scandal. A debate ensued over his suitability to lead the party and the result was a disastrous split in allegiances, with two distinctive groups, Parnellites and anti-Parnellites, developing.

The GAA were embroiled in the row, as a great many of the Association's members were also Home Rule members. When voting on the future of Parnell took place, leading GAA officials were found to be on opposing sides. With the widening of the split in the Home Rule movement, an inevitable struggle for control of the nationalist movement ensued. The GAA, as a body, despite the non-complicity of some members, supported Parnell resolutely. Were politics now becoming more important to the GAA than its own health as a sporting body?

The GAA's support for Parnell would alienate it from the clergy, the Home Rule movement and others, threatening its very existence, and placing it in a crisis from which it would take a decade to recover. Parnell's decision to marry the then divorced O'Shea in 1891 increased his unpopularity and ensured a total loss of the influential clergy's support for him. Parnell died in 1891, with the GAA staunchly supporting him to the end. It was not by then a popular stance. Members left the Association in droves. Clubs went out of existence and competitions suffered. Indeed, in whole counties the GAA died.

Yet the Association would fight back. The resilience of individual leaders helped offset a calamitous total disintegration. It was sheer hard work on their part that brought the GAA back from the grave. The hold the native games had on the Irish no doubt tugged at the hearts of many rank-and-file people too. The revival was boosted by the establishment of the Gaelic League, a cultural body many of whose members would join the GAA, conscious that the two associations shared common nationalist-minded objectives.

By the end of the nineteenth century, the GAA had recovered the ground it lost during the Parnell split. The bitterness had begun to disappear. The Gaelic League had helped to foster a new united desire for the promotion of nationalist ideals. On the playing fields, the games were again progressing well. Now just sixteen years old, the GAA had much to be proud of, not least its unwavering resilience. Most importantly, Ireland's natives games had been successfully revived, and the people's spirits lifted. A national movement had indeed been born.

2
—

THE GAA IN THE TWENTIETH CENTURY

By the early twentieth century the GAA's games had evolved
further from the old rough-and-tumble days; the chaotic
versions of centuries before were gone for ever. Players were
now using their imagination and guile, much to the dis-
appointment of wrestling enthusiasts.

The 1916 Rising, when the Irish rebelled against English
rule, had a seriously disruptive effect on the GAA's games
(see Chapter 10), but once a semblance of political stability
had returned, they continued to flourish. This is typical of
the history of the GAA, which has always managed to recover
from crisis and is justifiably proud of its capacity to do so.
Two World Wars merely slowed its progress.

The GAA was faced with a new Ireland in 1923, after the
partition of the country and the civil war. The Association
took some time to recover from the hostilities, in which GAA
rank-and-file members were at the coalface.

On a practical level, its games had been disrupted, with
some counties slow to recover from the devastating war that
had seen members of the same family fight on opposite
sides. Recover they did, however, and slowly the games began
to rise in quality and popularity.

To win the premier hurling and football competition, the

Senior All-Ireland, became the most sought-after sporting prize available to Irishmen. In the All-Irelands, county teams compete firstly in their own provincial sections; then come the All-Ireland semi-finals, where the provincial champions meet. The semi-finals and final are played at Croke Park.

In 1927 the Sam Maguire Cup was awarded for the first time to the captain of the winners of the All-Ireland football final. It has been presented to every winning captain since. Sam Maguire was a Cork Protestant who made an outstanding contribution to the GAA and whose memory lives on through his association with the great championship. The winners of the All-Ireland hurling championship receive the Liam McCarthy Cup, a trophy first played for in 1923 when Limerick defeated Dublin in what was actually the delayed 1921 final! That Cup finally gave in to Father Time in 1992 and was replaced by a new McCarthy Cup. Liam McCarthy was actually born in England, of Irish parents. He was a tremendous worker for the GAA in London and presented the Cup to the Association in appreciation of the work it was doing for young people and in the hope that it would stimulate interest in hurling.

THE TELEVISION AGE

Throughout the 1930s, 1940s and 1950s, standards continued to rise, attendances at big matches soared and the numbers playing grew dramatically. The GAA had become a sporting and cultural phenomenon, and had taken a firm foothold in the life of the country. Every parish had a club and virtually every household had some input into that club.

In the early 1960s the game's profile was boosted further by the arrival of television. Initially this had an adverse effect on the Association, with attendances at matches dropping considerably. However, it soon began to play a positive role for Gaelic games. Along with radio, the new broadcasting medium brought the excitement of top matches to virtually every household in the country, creating great publicity for the GAA and leading thousands of teenage boys to daydream about emulating the heroes whose magical feats they were hearing and seeing so much of.

The arrival of television coincided with the historic breakthrough in football by Down, whose emotional 1960 All-Ireland win saw the Sam Maguire Cup cross the border for the first time. Down's victory increased interest in Gaelic football in the North. New success by any county is usually welcomed, breathing new life into the games while leading to improved standards and competitiveness.

THE SHORT HANDPASS

The GAA success story continued throughout the swinging sixties and the not-so-swinging seventies. During this period Gaelic football underwent a radical change, with a new style, the short handpassing or running game, being developed. This new emphasis on passing the ball by the hand in slick moves was in sharp contrast to the traditional 'catch and kick' style.

The roots of the hand pass can be traced back to the 1960s, as more and more thought was invested in Gaelic football. The game was becoming marginally more sophisticated with each passing year. Certain counties developed their own variations on how they played the game. In Down the introduction of modern coaching techniques was supported by a major emphasis on physical fitness, and the county was rewarded with three All-Irelands in that decade. The Galway team that shared the football plaudits with Down in the 1960s – winning three successive All-Irelands – also introduced exciting new concepts of forward play.

In the early 1970s, Dublin, inspired by their manager Kevin Heffernan, brought these new concepts a stage further. Heffernan revolutionised the approach to training, introducing innovative and fiercely demanding new training techniques, previously unknown in Gaelic football. As amateurs, Gaelic footballers trained a couple of evenings a week; it was all that work and family commitments would allow. Heffernan also placed a major emphasis on the short-passing style, which, once perfected, complimented the speed and fitness levels of his players. It made Dublin an awesome force.

Kerry, managed by the equally thoughtful Mick O'Dwyer, responded to the challenge. Kerry had always been associated with great fielding of the ball and the catch and kick philosophy. O'Dwyer changed this approach in his pursuit of glory. The team matched Dublin's revolutionary new training schedules and adopted the short-passing game to devastating effect. Players no longer stayed in their positions, and forwards in particular employed off-the-ball running tactics that frustrated defences. Players in general formed running groups on the field, passing the ball to one another over short distances, dispensing with the simplistic catch and kick approach. The game had been changed forever.

Kerry continued to catch and kick, of course, but combined the traditional style with the short handpassing approach, which perfectly suited their speedy, intelligent forwards. Their quick mastery of the new style produced many memorable goals as opposing defences struggled to deal with the speed of foot, hand and thought exhibited by Kerry.

The great Kerry football team graced the 1970s and 1980s, winning eight All-Irelands, while their rivals, Dublin, won three in the 1970s. The emergence of Dublin as a force helped to revitalise interest in the game in the capital. It was a significant boost for the Association, as its games had frequently struggled to prosper in the city.

Meanwhile the GAA's headquarters at Croke Park in Dublin was consistently upgraded, just as stadiums and general facilities throughout the country were constantly improving.

THE 1980s AND 1990s

In the 1980s and 1990s the Association has gone from strength to strength. It now has almost 800,000 members (almost 25 per cent of the population) and 2,700 clubs, with over 20,000 teams between them. The two main competitions for football and hurling are the championship and the league. Clubs in each county enter teams in the county championship and county league. The winners of the county championship then go forward to represent the county in the provincial championships and later in an All-Ireland club championship. In the county championships neighbouring clubs often develop rivalries so intense that in many cases ordinary GAA folk have more interest in their club's exploits than their county's. County teams are made up of top club players.

There are various grades, designed for different age groups and different standards. At inter-county level, there are competitions for all ages too. While the All-Ireland titles are by far the most coveted, the second most important are the national leagues. These (hurling and football) are played on a league basis, with the finals, like the All-Irelands, played in Croke Park. Similar competitive structures are in place for school and college teams.

National (primary) and secondary (post-primary) schools play in their own schools county championships, progressing to provincial and All-Ireland finals, ensuring that the schools are a magnificent breeding ground for footballers of the future and that Gaelic games play a pivotal role in the development of the country's youth.

The colleges structure is equally impressive. The first colleges All-Ireland competition, also run on a provincial basis, was played for in 1911. In the same year the university football competition was introduced, with the winners claiming the prestigious Sigerson Cup. Its hurling equivalent is the Fitzgibbon Cup, introduced in 1912. These university and college championships ensure that young hurlers and footballers stay in touch with the game and are prepared for possible inter-county careers when they take their places as the men of the country.

The Railway Cup was an extremely popular competition in football and hurling, in which teams representing the four provinces met. First introduced in 1927, the Railway Cup hurling and football finals were played on St Patrick's Day and attracted enormous crowds in the early days, but gradually diminished in popularity and are gone off the rails, so to speak, in the modern era. A contributory factor to their decline has been the growth in popularity of the All-Ireland club championship, the progress of the local team being more important to fans than that of the provincial representatives. Once seen as a coveted competition because county players were receiving the honour of being selected for their pro-vince, the Railway Cup has suffered a collapse in popularity that is sad but seemingly irreversible.

The GAA established an awards system in 1971, with players in hurling and football receiving All-Star awards as members of a specially selected team of the season.

THE GAA DIASPORA

Virtually anywhere that Irish people have settled abroad, GAA clubs have developed. They provide Irish emigrants with a real sense of still belonging to Ireland and the GAA. The GAA clubs abroad keep the Irish there in touch with their heritage and their culture. In England and Scotland there are well over one hundred GAA clubs in existence. Over thirty have been established in Australia and a dozen or so in Canada.

In the United States, where Irish emigrants have played the GAA's games since the formation of the Association, Gaelic games are now played competitively by large numbers, with over one hundred clubs in existence and the games run under the auspices of the North American and New York Boards.

Star players from Ireland have traditionally gone to the United States in the summer months and played for clubs there in the local championship. Unfortunately, they were never meant to, at least not unless certain criteria were met. Where rules have been breached the GAA generally imposes bans, but the tradition continues amid suspicions that players are being offered financial inducements to play in the US.

The football authorities in the United States have had an uneasy relationship with the GAA in Dublin, who, ultimately, are their masters. Occasional controversies and fits of temper aside, the contribution of the GAA in Ireland to the GAA in America and that of the GAA in America to the GAA in Ireland – if you follow – have been important.

A CULTURAL ROLE

The Association has meanwhile made a significant contribution to the social development of the country through its advocacy of community leisure and cultural activity.

In the 1960s the vision and initiative of then GAA General

Secretary Padraig Ó Caoimh resulted in the establishment of Scor competitions. The Irish word *scor* means talent, and the Gaelic Athletic Association's Scor competitions are therefore talent contests, held as an annual showpiece for amateurs. In addition to the senior Scor, 'Scor na nÓg' is held for the young members of the GAA.

They were set up as an acknowledgement by the GAA that it had an obligation to contribute in a meaningful way to the social and cultural development of its vast membership. Scor would bind the GAA family together, while maintaining the popularity of traditional Irish music and song, and of course the Irish language, to which the Association is naturally committed. There are various Scor categories, such as Singing, Recitation, Novelty Act, Dancing and Music. Only GAA clubs are eligible to enter Scor competitions. County Scor finals are held, with clubs entering teams in the various categories. Provincial and All-Ireland finals follow.

The GAA retains its amateur status, if only just. Players are still unpaid, although they receive expenses, and top stars are increasingly being tempted by attractive sponsorship deals, involving, for example, their endorsement of products.

Today the Association so humbly founded in Hayes's Hotel has a profound influence on Irish life and on the lives of Irish people everywhere. It is an enormously successful sporting body that has taken on oppression, famine, wars, emigration, detractors and rival sports. It has always been in the same league as the Catholic Church in terms of its influence – these days the once enormous influence of the Church in Ireland is waning somewhat, but the GAA's remains strong. It is, in every sense, a national movement.

Football is played all over the country, participated in or watched by just about every second household. Hurling is slowly spreading to new counties, if not nearly as widely played as football. Extremely strong in its traditional strong-holds, the ancient game is enjoying a high profile through exciting television exposure, but the GAA will be anxious in the years ahead to see it develop further in parts of the country where it is currently weak. Handball and camogie are quite popular, with improved facilities for the former helping to attract new players. Ladies have joined the mass parti-cipation in and support for the native games in substantial numbers.

The GAA has succeeded spectacularly in preserving Ireland's native games, while seeing off the perceived threat from English influence. Its nationalist leanings have also made an impact. It has succeeded in uniting the people, at least in spirit, through its definition of Irishness. All over the world, people of Irish extraction identify with each other and the 'homeland' through the GAA. On the negative side, many non-Catholics and non-nationalists feel that the Association is too inward-looking, even sectarian. Its insistence that members of the British security forces remain banned from playing its games infuriates Protestants and is seen as small-minded. With the political future of Northern Ireland at yet another crossroads, it is an issue that the GAA will have to address in the near future.

The Gaelic Athletic Association's founder, Michael Cusack, died in 1906. Today, at Croke Park, the GAA's leading ground, the magnificent new Cusack Stand is a fitting visual tribute to the man who, with the help of others, showed the way. No doubt on All-Ireland final day, with thousands in the Cusack Stand and millions worldwide watching on television, the sod he loved dearly rests gently on the founder of the Gaelic Athletic Association. Ireland, truly, has embraced Michael Cusack's dream.

3

GAELIC FOOTBALL

Michael Cusack is dead, and so are the generations of people who played Gaelic football and hurling in their various primitive forms throughout the centuries. Quite what those who played football would make of the modern sophisticated game, we can only guess. It has certainly evolved greatly from its wild origins. For a start, they don't use human heads for balls any more. Animals no longer run for cover if they suspect that a game is about to start, as the days of hundreds of players brawling their way across the fields are long gone.

Refined and improved throughout the years, Ireland's national game is now a sophisticated sport which, when played with imagination and in a free-flowing manner, can be beautiful to watch. When it reaches its heights, it easily compares with any field game in the world. From its primitive origins it has developed into an exciting physical contact sport of which the Irish are understandably proud.

Once the GAA was established, the drive to introduce much-needed order to Gaelic football began. The sport had slowly evolved from the days of cross-country games and was now being played on pitches, but teams were uneven in size, rules minimal and rough play still prevalent.

In 1886, two years after it had been founded, the GAA

introduced football rules which helped detach the game forever from its rough-and-tumble past. Teams were now restricted to playing no less than fourteen players and no more than twenty-one, with the numbers to be agreed upon between the two opposing captains before a game. A football pitch was to be at least 120 yards long and 80 wide. The goals were 15 feet across, with a crossbar 8 feet off the ground. The only form of scoring was goals, which were awarded when the ball went under the crossbar. The duration of a game was one hour.

Soon points were introduced. Two point-posts or uprights were positioned twenty-one feet from the goal (one on either side). When the ball passed inside these posts or over the crossbar a point was awarded. In the early days a game was won by the team that scored the most goals, with points being irrelevant unless no goals were scored or both teams scored the same number of goals.

FOOTBALL TODAY

Football is now played by two fifteen-a-side teams. There have been many other changes over the years. The pitch is now 130 metres (minimum) to 145 metres (maximum) in length, and 80 to 90 metres in width. At either end of the pitch there are two goalposts which are 6.5 metres apart and are situated in the centre of the endline. They are a minimum of 7 metres in height with a crossbar fixed to the goalposts at a height of 2.5 metres above the ground.

The two forms of scoring remain goals and points, with a goal having the value of three points. A game is now won by the team with the greater total score (from either goals or points) at the end of the game. Thus a team that scores 1-3 (one goal and three points) has a total of six points and would defeat a team on 1-2 (a goal and two points) or 0-5

The Field of Play for
Gaelic Football and Hurling

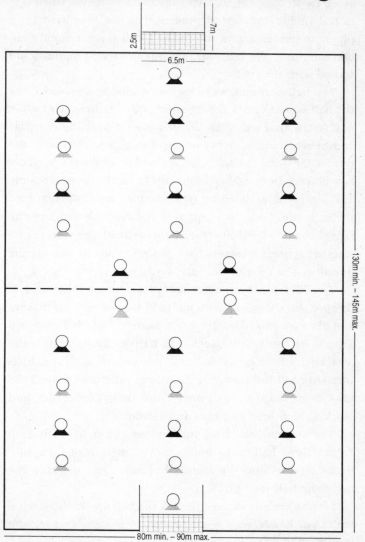

2.5m

7m

6.5m

130m min. – 145m max.

80m min. – 90m max.

• Not to scale

(five points). Most goals are kicked, but it is permissible to score by striking the ball with the hand or hands when it is in full flight. However, at present it is not permitted for a player in possession to fist the ball into the net. Points can be fisted over the crossbar, although the vast majority are scored with the foot.

The ball is round, as in soccer. A goal is awarded when the ball is sent under the crossbar (again as in soccer) while points are awarded when the ball is sent over the crossbar and between the uprights or posts. A game starts with the referee throwing the ball up in the middle of the pitch, where two players from each side line up to battle for possession. The referee is assisted by two linesmen and four umpires, the men who dress like butchers and risk the wrath of the fans as they adjudicate (for the benefit of the referee) on whether scoring attempts have passed inside or outside the uprights. The referee has final say.

The fifteen players on a team line out as follows: goalkeeper, six defenders, two midfield (or centrefield) players and six forwards. The defensive sextet is divided into two groups of three, full-backs and half-backs. Likewise, the attacking sextet is divided into two groups of three, half-forwards and full-forwards. The three full-backs defend the area nearest their goal, protecting their goalkeeper and marking the three opposing full-forwards.

The system continues further out the field, with each team's three half-backs lining across in front of their full-backs (and behind the midfield players) and marking the opposing half-forwards.

Players are not allowed to pick the ball up off the ground with their hands, with the exception of the goalkeeper, who is allowed to do so in a specifically marked area near his goal. The other players must either catch the ball before it reaches the ground or flick it into their hands with their feet. When the ball is not on the ground, it can be played with any part of the body.

The ball is passed to team-mates either by kicking, handpassing or fisting. Throwing the ball is not allowed. A handpass has to involve a definitive striking action. The essential difference between Gaelic football and soccer (apart from the scoring system) is of course that in Gaelic football all fifteen players can handle the ball. However, unlike in rugby, the players are not allowed to carry the ball at will. They must observe certain rules while carrying the ball in their hands or have a free-kick awarded against them.

Players can carry the ball in their hand for four paces, at which point they must release the ball or engage in a solo run. The 'solo' is the transfer of the ball from 'toe to hand' while on the run. During the solo the ball may be bounced once, and once after each transfer of it from toe to hand. It is one of the great skills of Gaelic football and the sight of a top player, such as Kerry legend Pat Spillane, in full flight on a solo run is one of the game's great spectacles.

Points are far more common than goals, as they are much easier to score. Games are sometimes won on points alone. Championship games (the premier competitions) are played over seventy minutes, while league games last for an hour.

As the game evolved over the years it became more scientific, with less emphasis on physical aggression and more on ball skills and coordinated team movements.

Gaelic football, however, remains a very physical game. In fact, this is part of its great appeal. It is one of the ultimate physical contact sports. When a player is in possession of the ball he can expect his 'marker' – his direct opponent who 'shadows' him for most of the game – to try to dispossess him, generally using as much physical force as the rules permit (and frequently more).

Often a player will be tackled by more than one opponent, with his marker assisted by a team-mate. To outsiders the physical nature of these tackles can seem brutal, but they are much more refined than in the past, are accepted as a vital part of the game by the players, and in most instances are loved by the fans.

The unfortunate player in possession can expect a great deal of physical contact with his marker. Players are pulled and dragged, shoulder-charged, grappled with and pushed. The shoulder-charging is actually allowed, but the other attentions are not. Sometimes homage is paid to the game's origins, and punches are thrown, with full-scale fist-fights ensuing. You can almost hear the ghosts of previous generations chanting in eerie approval.

You might feel that at this stage the referee should have stepped into action or that, in outlining the physical contact dimension of Gaelic football, I have confused what is permitted and what is not.

It is not so simple. One of the great dilemmas facing Gaelic football is the continued absence of a clear definition of what is a legitimate tackle. Yes, shoulder-charging is permitted and fist-fighting is not, but there is a grey area between what is considered acceptable and what isn't. The players of course occupy that area!

Referees obviously call a halt to any outbreak of fighting but they differ, in accordance with human nature, in their attitudes to the pushing, pulling and grappling. Because there is no agreed definition of the tackle, the actions of players are subject to the interpretations of the given referee. Thus, one referee might allow a player to make contact with his opponent all over his upper body, while another might have cautioned him for the first inkling of an offence. The first referee will be called lenient. The second might be called a no-nonsense referee by the media – and something more colourful by angry fans.

There are, not surprisingly, recurring complaints that the GAA has a problem with inconsistent refereeing; but the real problem is that the Association does not have a defined tackle in Gaelic football.

Of course, since the physical contact aspect of the game is one of the main reasons for its popularity, if physical contact was banned, thereby removing the confusion over what is and what isn't a legitimate tackle, much of the excitement and attraction of the game would be lost.

FIELDING

Another traditional attraction has been spectacularly high 'fielding' by players. 'Fielding' is the word used to describe arguably the most thrilling feature of the game. A player is fielding the ball when he rises off the ground to catch it with both hands after it has been kicked. The most spectacular form of fielding is obviously when a player leaps to a great height, and does so despite the challenge of opponents vying with him for the ball.

While fielding can take place in any part of the field, it is an art traditionally centred around goalkeepers' kick-outs. The best fielders on a team are usually the two midfield players. As the goalkeeper prepares to restart play with his kick-out, the four midfield players (two from each team) position themselves where they think the ball is likely to drop. With due jostling for position as the ball is in the air, they then rise from the ground and the best man wins possession, usually to an approving roar from the crowd.

This, at least, is how it used to be. Fielding was always a key part of Gaelic football, with high fielding by midfield players the highlight of games. However, in the modern era, with players now much fitter and faster than their predecessors, the game has changed. In years gone by, the high-fielding midfield player was arguably the team's most important figure. By winning the ball from the opposing team's kick-out he was regaining possession for his side and setting them on the attack again.

In those days tactics and sophisticated attacking strategies barely existed and the high-fielding midfield player would make use of possession by kicking the ball straight back towards the opposition goal. Hence the term 'catch and kick', which over the years has become a label for the traditional style of Gaelic football.

CATCH AND KICK

As we have seen, up to the 1960s and 1970s, Gaelic football was generally played in the catch and kick style. Players caught the ball and kicked it. Simple and direct. Now, with its new sophisticated approach, the game has other labels, such as the 'short-passing' or 'running' game, in which teams try to retain possession of the ball through a succession of handpasses over short distances.

Nowadays, high fielding and the catch and kick philosophy are employed less and less. Elaborate training routines, unheard of in the past, and fitter players have brought about a revolution in how the game is played.

Fielding is still a feature of the game, but in the midfield area players now tend to 'break the ball', i.e. punch or palm it away from opponents in the hope that waiting team-mates will catch it. Breaking the ball is easier than trying to field it cleanly and it is considered a necessary tactic because the midfield area is now much more congested than in the past.

The reason for that congestion is, again, that there have

been changes in the pattern of the game. In the old days players stayed in their positions for the entire game. A full-back certainly wouldn't see his full-forward until the match was over – if they weren't on talking terms he mightn't see him all year.

Now, with improved fitness and new tactics, defenders freely move forward to assist their attacking players, and forwards appear all over the pitch either in search of the ball or to help out their defence. The midfield area has become, in the words of legendary Irish sports columnist Con Houlihan, like O'Connell Street in Dublin on a busy Friday afternoon. The area that was once the hallowed ground in which great midfielders exhibited their graceful high-fielding skills has now become the place where all the players hang out.

Whether changes in the game have improved it or not is a matter of opinion. Undoubtedly, the faster version of the current era can be wonderfully exciting when two evenly matched teams meet and produce a fast, thunderous, physical encounter. Gaelic football has retained its capacity to excite and thrill. However, many traditionalists resent the fact that so many modern teams have partly abandoned the catch and kick approach. They feel today's players are disloyal to the game's roots. Indeed it is likely that if they were alive today some of those who were in the GAA in its infancy would be appalled at the use of the handpass at all. A directive towards the end of the nineteenth century pleaded with players in a particular area not to carry the ball, or pass it, as they were merely 'borrowing from rugby'. Instead, they were urged just to kick it.

The short handpassing approach is dismissed as 'basket-ball', and many of the traditionalists side with the so-called lenient referees in the belief that the use of more physical strength should be allowed. The breaking of the ball, at the expense of fielding, is viewed by this group as a further change for the worse.

There are others who believe that Gaelic football is improving. They appear to be in a minority, however. They argue that the game is faster and therefore more exciting. The short-passing game is good to watch, and, they point out, the catch and kick technique is still in use, just to a lesser degree than before.

Ultimately, each fan must make up his or her own mind on whether the changing game is superior or inferior to the versions that preceded it. What cannot be disputed is that Gaelic football has grown in popularity, and even if we witness many disappointing games season after season, attendances continue to rise and public interest is enormous. The occasional classic game, in any event, reminds us all of how special Gaelic football is, whatever its weaknesses.

Interestingly, while Gaelic football, even at its best, is regarded by many as an inferior game to hurling – in 'hurling country' they will insist that their game is superior to anything on God's earth, black pudding and Guinness included – it is by far the most widely played of the GAA games. For every hurler, there are many footballers. The game is played at countless levels in every parish in the Republic and Northern Ireland. It is reasonable to ask why football is more popular than hurling, if the accepted wisdom is that hurling is more skilful and thrilling.

Again, tradition provides the answer. Top-class hurling has historically been confined to particular parts of the country, such as Kilkenny, Cork and Tipperary. Football spread more easily. One simple explanation for that might be a lack of availability of hurleys or sticks. A football, or a substitute for a football (preferably not a human head), could always be found. Hurleys would not have been so easily made or, when they became more sophisticated, purchased.

The reality is that football has always been the most accessible of the GAA's two big games. The four-year-old child is more likely to get his hands on an old football than an old hurley. Then the love affair has begun.

Maybe football's greater popularity can be linked too to groups of schoolchildren walking home from school in that less-than-direct manner that they have mastered. If the odd football is not lying around on the route, a few stones or perhaps an empty can will invite a kick and inspire dreams of Croke Park, or even Wembley. The sight of youngsters striking a ball with a hurley as they set off for school is common only in the traditional hurling strongholds.

Sons tend to play the games their fathers played or told them about. A small boy wide-eyed with wonder at tales of the feats of football legends like Mick O'Connell will demand a new football in preference to a hurley.

Gaelic football is therefore in the healthy state it's in largely because its roots are so widespread. Only County Kilkenny opt not to enter the All-Ireland football championships (because their obsession with hurling has prevented the development of a good county team). Every other county sends its team out each year in search of Gaelic football's greatest prize, the All-Ireland title. The various club competitions meanwhile are contested with a fierce passion and enthusiasm.

The game is also very strong in the schools, despite the counter-attraction presented by other sports, most obviously soccer. Most young boys with any potential as players will be nurtured at school or in their local club, and such is the solidity of the GAA's roots throughout Ireland that few are lost to the game.

The counties that have dominated Gaelic football most are

Kerry and Dublin. They have won fifty-three of the one hundred and ten All-Irelands held up to 1997 (there was no championship in 1888). Kerry have triumphed a record thirty-one times, compared to Dublin's twenty-two successes. Others that have traditionally been powers in the game include Cork, Galway, Meath, Cavan and Down. Leinster and Munster have been the strongest provinces, but Ulster and Connacht have had their great teams too.

Throughout the years, the people have remained loyal to the most widely played of the Gaelic games. The love affair between the Irish and the game they've nurtured through the ages shows no sign of wilting. Neither party is bored. The excitement remains. In thousands of pubs across Ireland every week men and women cheer on the giants of English soccer on Sky Sports. The fun and the escapism generally ends after ninety minutes and a few action-replays. Then the plumbers and farmers and barbers and shopkeepers dispense with the soccer, fond of it as they are, and return to the real world. Family life, mortgages, work, bills and the game next Sunday on the local GAA pitch.

Gaelic football. Catch and kick or short-passing. Catch and kick *and* short-passing. Or whatever. Fierce shoulder-charges, powerful men rising for a high ball, great goals and high lofted points; fast, furious action, pace, aggression, the unleashing of the week's tension in the desperate search to be the best. And the need to trudge off the field at the end, emptied of energy, but proud and fulfilled. Everything the Gaelic footballer has ever wanted.

4

HURLING

Very little in life is simple and straightforward. That the earth is round has been disputed. That there is a God is a view opposed by some. Was that Elvis himself, hale and hearty, that you saw crossing the street this morning?

If only it was all as straightforward as the stature of hurling is to the people who cherish Ireland's ancient, glorious game. It is their considered view, quite simply, that hurling is the greatest field game in the world. Having attended some wonderful All-Ireland semi-finals and finals, and watched other classic matches on television, it's a view that I share. Indisputable. Hurling takes your breath away.

No God? Bring an atheist to a hurling game. If it's even an average match, wink at him and get him thinking. If it's a classic, bring him for a pint and ask him, 'Now is there a God in heaven?'

There are many Irishmen and women who have had reason to link God with the game of hurling when it has been seen at its most exhilarating. Witnessed in all its majesty, hurling's boast that it is not just the fastest but also the most thrilling and skilful field game in the world takes on great credibility. When such superb displays take place, it must indeed do wonders for the faith of many.

What magic the great hurlers possess. The hurler in full flight silences the whispered protests of pretenders. No soccer or rugby player, or Gaelic footballer either, finds it easy to press his case when confronted with the hurler in motion. It is awesome, gracious and sublime.

To understand the great game, it is necessary to reflect again on its origins. As we saw earlier, the ancient game was reputedly played thousands of years ago, while in more recent centuries the Irish played the village-to-village and cross-country versions.

Being such an unusual game, hurling had many critics and was completely baffling to visitors. In the twelfth century the Norman invaders tried to ban it, but they failed, and eventually began to play the game themselves. In the 1600s the Gaelic chieftains had their own teams, and betting on games was widespread. Its life in England, though brief (in historical terms), was nonetheless colourful. The people of Cornwall and Devon had their own peculiar rules for the version of hurling they were playing towards the end of the sixteenth century. Teams of 'fifteen, twenty or thirty' began by stripping to their underwear and holding hands, a dubious start by any standards. It certainly wouldn't happen in Tipperary or Cork.

Two bushes acted as goals at either end, each being placed eight or ten feet apart, and each manned by 'a couple of the best stopping hurlers'. When the game started, the idea was to get the ball past the defiant duo. 'But therein consists a Herculean task,' noted the writer Richard Carew, as quoted in Joe Lennon's *The Playing Rules of Football and Hurling*. The man in possession, and an unfortunate man he was, was seemingly set upon by virtually all of the opposing players. He could, however, 'butt' them in return for their attentions. Butting was not the coarse act that it is today, favoured by the bully-boy and involving head-to-head contact; it was a simple matter of the player in possession thrusting at his opponent's chest with a closed fist. Charming.

It might have appeared that the man in possession was winning at this point, but when one or more of the opposition – those who weren't on their knees clutching their chests – finally grounded him, his persecution could only end by his touching the ground with some part of his body or by crying out 'Hold!' Butting, incidentally, was 'a symbol of manhood' according to Carew, and no doubt it was, especially coming from a man wearing little more than his underpants.

CAMÁNACHT AND IOMÁNAÍOCHT

Back in Ireland, there existed until modern times two distinctive forms of hurling, both of which were vying for supremacy. *Camánacht* was a form of ground-hurling, while hurling (*iománaíocht* in Irish) was the aerial version. *Camánacht* is no longer in existence in Ireland – it was more or less extinct by the time the GAA was set up – but it is still played in Scotland, where it is known as shinty. While the version of the game exclusively involving ground-hurling is gone, the modern game does incorporate this less popular style.

By the nineteenth century, a typical hurling game in Ireland involved a manageable fifty or sixty players, usually barefoot, who would do battle on a pitch. The play had no real pattern to it. 'Follow the ball, lads' was the hurling cry – and everyone did. Wherever the ball went, all the players followed. They showed great skill, however, and visiting observers were invariably amazed at what they saw.

While hurling was being played throughout Ireland in the late nineteenth century, hurley was the version then popular in Dublin. Hurley was a much 'softer' and less physical game than hurling, and similar to what we now know as hockey.

Michael Cusack greatly disapproved of it; he announced he would take steps to 're-establish the national game of hurling' which, as we noted earlier, he had seen and played in his native Clare.

When the GAA was formed in 1884, hurling, like football, became more organised and the great skills involved were allowed to flourish. Hurley was effectively ignored: ground-hurling was incorporated into the more exciting aerial hurling, or else allowed to peter out.

Over the years that followed the founding of the GAA, the 'new', somewhat refined version of hurling enthralled the Irish public. At the beginning of the twentieth century the game's popularity spread further. Young boys learnt the skills of hurling at an early age, devoting hours of practice to a game that takes a hypnotic hold of its new fans.

Like the generations who went before them, these young-sters mastered the various skills, growing into men whose prowess has made the twentieth century memorable for great hurling contests and wonderful individual expressions of the epic game.

Hurling is revered for many reasons, the most obvious of which is that there is nothing else quite like it. The game, whatever its variations, has always revolved around men striking a ball with a curved stick. This is what differentiates it from Gaelic football. As with football, it acquired important new regulations in 1886, with teams restricted in numbers and instructions issued regarding the size of pitches. Hurling posts were 20 feet apart with the crossbar 10 feet off the ground, and, as in football, for a brief period before the introduction of points, the only form of scoring was goals, which were awarded when the ball went under the crossbar. Later, points were introduced. Two point-posts or uprights were positioned 21 feet from the goal (one on either side).

When the ball passed inside these posts or over the crossbar, a point was awarded. In the early days, as in football, a game was won by the team that scored the most goals. Points were only relevant if both teams scored the same amount of goals or if no goals were scored, in which case the team with the most points were deemed the winners.

The modern-day game involves two teams of fifteen players battling it out on a pitch, each man equipped with a hurley. The pitch is now 130 metres (minimum) to 145 metres (maximum) in length, and 80 to 90 metres in width. The goal areas are the same as in Gaelic football. At either end of the pitch there are two goalposts which are 6.5 metres apart, situated in the centre of the endline. They are a minimum of 7 metres in height with a crossbar fixed to the goalposts at 2.5 metres above the ground.

The hurley, also known as the *camán*, is no doubt more impressive than the humble stick used over the centuries, but its function remains the same. It is made from ash wood, and is an inch over three feet in length. The handle is three and a half inches in width (except at the top where it is narrower) and the curved end (or '*bas*'), with which the ball is struck, is seven inches deep and five inches wide. The ball used is made of leather, is small and very hard, and is also known as the *sliotar*. It should have a circumference of not less than 23 and not more than 25 centimetres. In the old days the ball was made of cow's hair.

The object of the game is to score points and goals, as in Gaelic football. The team with the greater total number of points are deemed the winners. Thus a team with 2-10 (16 points in total) will defeat a team with 5-0 (15 points). A goal (where the ball is sent under the crossbar) is worth three points, while a single point is awarded when the ball is struck over the crossbar and between the uprights. A player can

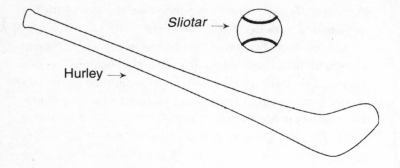

Sliotar →

Hurley →

score with his hand or hands only when striking a ball that is in full flight. He cannot score by throwing the ball when in possession. All other scores come when the ball is struck with the hurley.

The game starts when the referee throws in the ball in the centre of the pitch, with two players from each team lining up to contest possession. The ball may be struck when it is on the ground, in the air, tossed from the hand or lifted with the hurley. Players scoop the ball off the ground with the hurley or with the foot. They cannot use their hands to touch the ball on the ground or to pick it up. The ball cannot be thrown or carried in the hand for more than four paces. When tackling, a player must seek to take the ball from an opponent by using the hurley only, and there can be no contact with his hurley and the other player. Any strike of the ball can be referred to as a 'puck'.

As in football, the goalkeeper (a thankless role in hurling, because the ball is so small and moves so swiftly) is 'protected' by six defenders, while further upfield there are two midfielders and six forwards.

THE CLASH OF THE ASH

Unlike in the past, where everyone chased the ball endlessly, players now more or less stay in their positions, marking their direct opponent, and waiting for the action to come their way. Games last for seventy minutes in the major competition – the championship – and for sixty minutes in the league.

One of the reasons hurling is so exciting is the staggering speed at which the *sliotar* or ball travels. That alone would not be enough to make the game special if it were not supported by the range of exceptional skills the hurler possesses. The top players have a fantastic ability to score from long distances with sweet strikes of the ball; fans also marvel at their long, direct, accurate passes. The solo run shows off further impressive skills, with the hurler running at speed while holding the hurley at an angle that allows him to balance the ball as he runs. The player can carry the ball in the hand for a maximum of four consecutive steps or for no longer than the time needed to take four steps. A player may catch the ball, play it on his hurley and bring it back into his hand once.

There is an endless range of other skills. The one-handed catch requires timing, skill and bravery, with players rising above their opponents and flying hurleys to pluck the speeding *sliotar* from the air. Striking the ball is in itself a skill, years of practice being necessary before accuracy and the required power (for judging passes to colleagues) are perfected. Blocking is a marvellous skill whereby defending hurlers thwart an opponent as he is about to pass the ball or attempt a score. The block is made by timing to perfection the moment at which to divert the pass or attempted score with the hurley.

The result of the combination of these and other skills is a majestic game. The action starts when the referee throws in the ball – and all other games throw in the towel. Now the fire within thirty men is unleashed. The hurleys begin to dance and the ghosts of generations past smile in approval.

The battles are almost always riveting – a poor game of hurling is a rarity. The ball is moved from one end of the pitch to another at great speed, in the air and on the ground, with the action non-stop and the physical exchanges often fearsome. The man-to-man combat is sporting rivalry in all its naked beauty. The term 'the clash of the ash' sums up hurling at its best. It refers to that moment when the ash hurleys smack against each other – in desperate hope of connecting with the ball – and the sound that results. In more general terms of course, any hurling game is a 'clash of the ash'.

When a player connects with the ball on the ground this is called a ground-strike – a skill in itself, but not as exciting as the aerial combat. Battles for supremacy in the air are hurling's showpieces, with great athletes leaping to catch the ball cleanly – amidst flying hurleys – or often connecting beautifully as they strike the speeding ball in mid-air, helping it on its journey, indeed accelerating its progress, towards the opponents' goal. A fireball speeding through the air powered by Irish soul.

A great score in hurling, coming at the end of a sweeping move across the whole pitch, leaves the audience gasping. Sometimes the ball will not touch the ground for several moments; from player to player it travels, the nation watching, until finally someone finds a little space and directs it sweetly between the posts. The goalkeeper lines it up for the 'puck-out' (the term used for the restart of a game) and a new phase of exciting play begins.

Like Gaelic footballers, hurlers play the game for no monetary reward. While their dedication is tremendous, their courage is particularly deserving of recognition. Any fears about receiving blows seem to dissipate when the hurler, gladiator-like, takes to the field. Fired with a passion to succeed, hurlers show a willingness to embrace the battle which would shame the highly-paid stars of some other sports. Get first to the ball and accept the bruises that you pick up along the way; that is the philosophy.

While it is fiercely physical in nature, and a guaranteed provider of bruises, it would be wrong to depict hurling as an especially dangerous game. Hurling would be dangerous if it weren't played by hurlers. Played by boxers or snooker players, with no previous experience of the game, it would result in a long queue at the local casualty department.

However, the flying hurleys are generally in safe hands when the players concerned are experienced hurlers. It looks dangerous, but it isn't particularly so. Good hurlers, they say, aren't at risk in the midst of hurling battle. They know what's safe and acceptable. They have the split-second timing and the skills to ensure that something beautiful can emerge from what, to an outsider, looks like a wild scramble for possession of the ball.

Players do wear helmets – most do at least – because when things go wrong, hurling can lead to unfortunate injuries. Generally speaking, though, the game is played in a very sporting manner. Conscious that they are wielding potentially dangerous weapons, the players use them for the right reasons, and most injuries are caused accidentally.

The emphasis is on skill, and the game is in a healthier

state in this respect than Gaelic football, where increasingly the emphasis is on gaining physical supremacy over your opponents. In hurling, the top teams are intent on out-hurling each other, whereas in football, players often first try to psyche each other out by the use of physical force.

Indeed, hurling generally has the upper hand on football. The game is accepted by most – even ardent 'football men' – as being the greater of the two main GAA codes. The common view is that there is simply nothing to touch a hurling game when two great teams produce a classic contest featuring top players who display the unique skills of hurling at full speed. There are diehards who will say that football is a better game, but they are in a minority.

Yet hurling is played less widely than football, with fewer clubs having hurling than football teams. While the game is played to some standard in every county, hurling does not have deep roots in every part of the Republic or in areas of Northern Ireland. It is much stronger in its traditional strongholds, where they say hurlers are born, not coached. In these strong hurling areas the game is played with an incomparable passion. Pride means everything – defeat cannot be considered. Hurling is an enormous, integral part of the lives of these people. In some such areas a football would hardly be recognised – and if it was, it would probably be frowned upon.

The traditional hurling counties are Cork, Tipperary and Kilkenny. Wexford, Waterford and Limerick also have a proud hurling tradition. In these parts of Ireland, the people live and breathe the game. They are reared on stories of great feats by players who came from their area, including perhaps their fathers or other relatives. The young people are told dramatic tales of great battles between their village and the neighbouring one; from an early age they have the hurling obsession passed on to them. You might say babies in these regions are born, not with silver spoons in their mouths, but with crisp hurleys in their hands.

Tradition is our past, but it can play a part in shaping our future. Because of the men of yesterday, the men of tomorrow will hold hurleys too. The game is unlikely to die because it lives on in so many hearts. In the hurling strongholds, the schools further nurture the kids' fondness for the game they hear so much about at home. And so the cycle continues, with hurling's great message being spread by thousands of willing volunteers.

These counties, where the game has been strongest for centuries, invariably produce the best teams in the country. It is often said that each particular county produces players who have skills unique to that area.

The most successful hurling county of all is Cork. The Cork county team have won twenty-seven All-Irelands, with Kilkenny having won twenty-five and Tipperary third on the honours list, with twenty-four victories. Not surprisingly, the rest of the country has struggled to make an impression against these traditional hurling bases. However, a number of new powers in the game have emerged.

In the west, Galway made the breakthrough in the 1980s (they also won an All-Ireland in 1923), which was fitting given the game's long tradition there. In more recent years counties like Clare, Offaly and Wexford have emerged too, and in Ulster the progress made in Antrim has been welcomed.

There have been a few great hurling eras since the formation of the GAA but the general consensus is that the current era is the greatest of all. The emergence of more counties as forces in the game, while less than pleasing for some narrow-minded traditionalists, has led to a series of great championships.

Clare in particular have had the gall to prove that they can live with the best in Munster and Ireland. They had the distinction in 1997 of winning the first all-Munster All-Ireland final, when they defeated Tipperary. Normally the winners of the four provincial championships (in Connacht, Leinster, Munster and Ulster) contest the All-Ireland semi-finals but an experimental rule change had allowed runners-up in the Munster and Leinster championships to re-enter the All-Ireland, as competition is more intense in those provinces.

The emergence of these new powers is obviously a reflection on rising standards in those parts of the country. Thus, the whole championship gains; high standards attained by more teams lead to more great games. That has been the happy experience of fans in the 1990s.

Although there are some concerns about hurling's future health, in view of the threat posed by counter-attractions and the reality that the game has not spread to enough counties, Ireland's ancient game is enjoying the most exciting phase in its proud history. The GAA will need to work to develop the game at grassroots level, but in terms of thrilling matches and spectator interest, hurling is currently enjoying great health. This culture, this art, this way of Irish life, is flourishing. A country's individualism proudly exhibited. Amateurs playing arguably the greatest game in the world.

Every summer the crowds are gasping in Croke Park. Every Sunday the people of the parishes cheer on their local heroes. The young boys watch their fathers and dream that one day they will be masters in the clash of the ash. And, like their fathers and their grandfathers, they will.

5

HANDBALL

Take a leisurely drive through Ireland, and every so often you
are likely to come across one. A stern, imposing wall, about
eighteen feet in height, with two side-walls connected to it.
They appear in the countryside, as if from nowhere, large
cement peculiarities that are certainly not there as some
architectural addition to the area. Could it really be that these
walls were specially built so that men could spend endless
hours striking a tiny ball against them?

Indeed they were. These now largely isolated 'ball alleys'
are a reminder of the historic roots of the only GAA game
that has an international dimension. Handball is the simplest
of all the games of the Gaelic Athletic Association and one
that most of us can identify with. After all, although you may
never actually have played handball, what child has not had
a fascination with kicking or hitting a ball against a wall?

It is one of the first experiences we have of the magical
appeal of a ball and the magnetic attraction of sport. Hitting
a ball against the gable of our house. Trying to reach the
rebound. Having the audacity, as we improve, to aim for a
particular spot on the wall. A majority may never have been
in a handball alley or court (as it is also known), but the
world abounds with closet handballers.

The game involves two or four players (singles or doubles), a ball, durable hands and a few walls. Although there are variations in the size of court (60 feet x 30 feet and 40 x 20) and in the nature of the ball used, the basic object of the game is to defeat your opponent in a battle requiring speed, agility, guile and skill. Handball is like squash without the rackets, with the players striking the tiny ball against the front wall (later using the other walls), in the hope that they will place it where it eludes the opponent and thus deliver another point to the player who has 'served'.

Over the centuries the game was played in outdoor ball alleys (in the early days it was often played with just a single wall) but it has now become more sophisticated and moved indoors. Competition for both sexes and in all age groups now takes place in plush, enclosed handball courts, with a back wall added, making the game faster than ever and arguably more exciting.

The game has nothing like the status or appeal of football or hurling but it has always survived and frequently flourished in the limited circles in which it is popular. Uniquely among Gaelic games, it has a thriving international dimension, being played in the United States, Canada, Australia, Mexico, Spain and other parts of Europe. World and European championships are staged.

It is thought that Irish emigrants introduced the game to the United States and also to Australia, probably in the nineteenth century. US Army personnel were responsible for bringing it to Europe. Wherever it is played in the world, the various versions are all thought to be linked to the traditional Irish game, with the possible exception of 'Fives', a version that may have been peculiar to the United Kingdom, and 'Pelota', a game similar to handball, which is played in Spain.

Handball is easily described, which is not to say that it

is easily played, at least not to a high standard. The object of the game is to win each rally (exchange of shots) by serving or returning the ball so the opponent is unable to keep the ball in play. The ball is struck with the palm of the hand, or sometimes with a closed fist.

Before a game commences, there is a toss-up to see which player will have first service. A special service line is situated about halfway up the court. The server must stand between the service line and a so-called 'short-line', while the opponent takes up position outside the short-line. The server strikes the ball against the front wall, beginning the rally. If the opponent does not return the ball, an ace has been served, and the serving player has won the first point. More often a rally develops. Each contested rally that the server wins gains him or her a point; the opponent wins service when he or she wins a rally. This gives that player control of the game, as points can only be won on service. To lose serve is called a 'handout'.

A serve or rally is won when an opponent cannot return the ball to the front wall before it has touched the floor twice. The ball can rebound off any of the other walls or the ceiling in 40 x 20 competition; in 60 x 30 competition if one hits the ceiling a point is awarded or a handout (loss of service) ensues. The ball must be returned to the front wall either on the volley (without having touched the floor) or having bounced just once. The players bring the other walls into play, using them tactically, developing angled shots aimed at causing maximum problems for the opponent.

When a player has twenty-one points, he or she has won a game, and the player who is first to win two games wins the match. The duration of games therefore varies. A referee officiates at all competitive games.

Traditionally the Irish played with the hardball in open

courts. The hardball is about two inches in diameter, weighs about one and a half ounces, has a rubber centre and is bound with leather. The courts evolved into the present 60feet x 30 feet venues where hardball continues. Later the softball was introduced (this ball is about 2.2 inches in diameter, is made of rubber and weighs about 62 grammes) and this version of the game was played alongside the old hardball game. In recent decades the hardball code has declined, due mainly to a shortage of the skilled craftsmen needed to make hardballs. Overseas, particularly in the USA, the game introduced by the Irish took root. In the USA it evolved into what is now known as the 40 x 20 game or the International game. One, two and three-wall competitions are also played abroad. The 40 x 20 game was introduced into Ireland in the early 1970s, and a feature of this game is the use of the ceiling, making it in effect a five-wall game. Thus at the present time there are three handball codes played in Ireland, the traditional Irish game of 60 x 30 (hardball), softball (played in the 60 x 30 court) and 40 x 20 (the International game). Irish players have acquited themselves well in international competition, winning many US and world titles at various levels.

The history of handball is a proud one. The game has been played in Ireland since at least the eighteenth century and was probably played previously. In its formative years the game was occasionally played against just a front wall, usually by barefooted men. The ball was made from cowhair. Early in the game's development the referee was introduced, which was probably just as well, as players sometimes fought with each other.

Great champions, many of them wonderful showmen, sprung up all over Ireland, though mostly in Dublin or the south of Ireland, where the game was strongest. It was a major social occasion when visiting players came to take on the champion of an area. A town crier announced the impending game and a band would accompany both players to the court, where a large crowd would be in place to witness the protagonists engage in combat. Often some of the crowd would become noisy and unruly, presumably as the pressure grew; in those days it was usual for large bets to be placed on the outcome of games. This particular practice has died out; the Irish have not lost their fondness for placing bets but it is horses, greyhounds and occasionally football matches that attract the wagers (and too often the wages) these days.

There was a colour and excitement about handball in the era of those gladiatorial battles that does not exist now. The game had a style and showmanship about it which it has since lost, but this was probably inevitable in a changing world.

Handball had an international dimension as far back as one hundred years ago, making it the true pioneering game of the GAA. Towards the end of the nineteenth century a form of world championships were already being held by the enterprising stars of the day. Top players challenged one another for prize-money, making handball not just the GAA's only international sport, but its first professional one too! This phase of the game's history peaked between 1880 and 1909 with American and Irish players meeting in two-leg showdowns – one in America, one in Ireland – which, with some justification, they labelled world championships. Substantial sums of money were at stake, and the players were like prize-fighters, men with money on their mind, hustlers with handballs.

Meanwhile the GAA had been set up and, as one of Ireland's native games that was perceived to be under threat from foreign ones, handball came under the Association's wing. However, the game was largely ignored by the GAA from the outset. The lack of support from the Association would prove damaging to the game's development. Handball in fact went into predictable decline as team games grew in popularity. In many counties the game wasn't played at all. By 1910 the showdowns with the Americans before the large, enthralled crowds were no more.

The GAA finally did something about the game in 1923, when it ordered the establishment of provincial Handball Councils. The Irish Handball Council was set up the following year and was allowed to govern the game independently, although it remains a part of the GAA family.

As the new century grew, the game's fortunes were adversely affected again as it became an innocent victim of the speed with which the world was moving. With the arrival of cars and trains, people were able to travel in comfort and with ease to football and hurling matches. The loyal sojourn on foot to the local handball alley, far from being enticing, now seemed an outdated option.

Most Gaels had at best a minimal interest in this particular GAA code and its popularity remained in the hands – literally – of the dedicated few. The game was boosted in the 1940s thanks to the efforts of Corkman T. J. McElligott and others, who mastermined a revival of interest in handball which resulted in a new enthusiasm for the game across the country, with more facilities provided and more players taking up the game.

In the 1950s and 1960s came the timely renewal of interest in developing competition with the Americans and (in time) with players in other countries. The decision to compete internationally proved a major breakthrough for the game in Ireland and inspired the building of numerous new alleys to coincide with the accommodation of the 40 x 20 American version of the game.

OUTSTANDING PLAYERS

Throughout the years there have been many great handball players, and in the old days the game was full of characters – wonderfully gifted athletes who brought a sense of fun and showmanship to the game.

William Baggs from Tipperary might have escaped from a circus when young, so extrovert a showman was he. Baggs was unbeatable at the game when at his peak in the middle of the nineteenth century, and took to giving exhibitions in which he struck the ball with the soles of his feet, his hands tied behind his back. He defeated many opponents in this fashion!

There have been many outstanding exponents of the game in the years since. A legend of the game was the boy wonder Tom Jones, who beat every top player in Ireland in a spectacular reign during which he remained unbeaten. Tom Jones then became Fr Tom Jones, never playing competitively again after his ordination (for which his beleaguered opponents no doubt thanked God). The first great champion of the twentieth century meanwhile was John Joe Bowles from Limerick, who was Irish champion for seventeen years up to the early 1920s.

In his book *The GAA in Its Time*, Padraig Purcell quotes a description of Bowles: 'Down by the Shannon he appeared – a tall slender boy with fingers like a violinist and limbs like a ballet dancer.' In their own way, Bowles's feats were as remarkable as William Baggs's feet, but without wishing to take from either of them – certainly not from a man who could play handball with the considerable disadvantage of having his hands tied behind his back – it should be said that not many counties had taken up the game at that time.

Another star of the early part of the twentieth century was Oliver Drew of Cork. Paddy Perry from County Roscommon might be considered the first great champion of truly competitive times. He won eight All-Ireland senior softball titles in succession, from 1930 to 1937.

There were no All-Ireland softball championships held between 1942 and 1945, as there was a 'scarcity of softballs'. Presumably all complaints were to be dispatched to Mr A. Hitler. The war also dented progress for the great John Joe Gilmartin from County Kilkenny, who won seven All-Ireland senior hardball titles between 1936 and 1942 and would surely have added a few more had the war not interrupted his career. However, he returned in 1945 to add three further titles.

John Ryan of Wexford was the star of the 1950s, while Joe Maher of Louth enjoyed great success in the 1960s. Pat Kirby from County Clare won four All-Ireland senior softball singles titles in the 1970s and was one of the greatest players in the history of the game. He also dominated the 40x20. version when the 'American-size' game was played at All-Ireland level for the first time (in 1975), with Kirby winning the first six championships. The most famous player of modern times is undoubtedly Michael 'Duxie' Walsh, the Kilkenny wizard who has won thirteen consecutive All-Ireland senior softball titles in an incredible period of dominance.

Today the game is played in every county in Ireland. Each county has its own Handball County Board, and ladies have their own Board. County championships are keenly contested, and provincial championships and All-Irelands follow, with the finals held in Croke Park in the same month as the hurling and football showpieces.

Children usually take up the game at about ten years of

age, and in the past twenty years or so there has been a huge increase in the number of girls playing the game. Women's handball first became popular in the late 1950s, and is played to a high standard by a large number of girls and women today.

One of handball's great appeals is that it can be played to middle age and beyond. Many middle-aged or elderly people use it as a pastime and as a way to stay fit and healthy. In 1967 the first All-Ireland championships for Masters (over-forties) was played, and fifteen years later a Golden Masters competition, for over-fifties, was added to the growing fixture list. Later again, competition at over fifty-five and sixty years developed. In the United States there is a special championship for over-seventies.

Today, boosted by modern facilities, better organisation, some interest from television, and its international dimension, handball is a very competitive sport in Ireland. The magnificent new indoor facilities, in which all competition now takes place, have attracted more players, male and female, and the game is currently in a healthy state. The simple technique of making the back wall in the enclosed courts a see-through one with a glass panel has proven a great success, attracting spectators who can sit in comfort in sports centres, watching competitors in action.

Meanwhile, if you do take that drive around Ireland, you will notice that most of the old ball alleys are now desolate and deserted, showing the signs of years of neglect, the result of the apathy of the people and the rebirth of the game in its new indoor home. Handball, like so much else in life, has moved on, taking a step indoors, into warmth, comfort and sophistication. Spare a thought, though, as you pass the relics of a different age. We should look on the alleys with respect and think of the dancing stars of the past who kept the game breathing in the open countryside all those decades ago.

As is the GAA trademark, the game has survived and indeed grown. Who knows what the future will bring for handball? Despite the international competition, the future of the game should not be taken for granted, especially when one thinks of its struggles in the past. But then, as long as houses have something resembling gables, where the seeds of love are sown, it will probably be safe.

6

THE ROLE OF WOMEN IN THE GAA

Traditionally, women did not make the headlines in the GAA
– they made the tea. Happily, that is changing. Recent years
have seen a dramatic increase in the involvement of women
in Ireland's premier sporting body. Women now enjoy a
higher profile in the Association, both as participants in the
games and in the area of administration (though progress
here has been slower).

Ladies' football has become very popular, while camogie,
the GAA code exclusive to women, is currently thriving. The
administrative rise is indeed slow, but it is taking place, and
looks certain to accelerate. By tradition, women's primary
involvement in the GAA has been in a supporting role to the
menfolk, but nowadays 'GAA women' are no longer automatically assumed to be experts only in making sandwiches
and keeping football kits clean.

The ladies have donned those kits and joined in the action
on the field. Numerous ladies' football clubs have been
formed and all counties with the exception of Kilkenny
compete in the All-Ireland ladies' football championship.
Ladies do not play hurling, camogie being essentially a
version of hurling for women. Handball has long been a sport
played by both sexes.

On an administrative level, women now hold positions within clubs and on County Boards, and in the near future we can expect more and more female office-holders to rise up the administrative ladder and bring their skills and talents to the GAA's chambers of power. If and when this does happen, it will signal a remarkable transformation for the GAA. The Association has always been male-dominated and has arguably given the impression that it was perfectly at ease with this massive imbalance.

CAMOGIE

Women have long played camogie, for the very good reason that it is a women's game. The game was invented with the purpose of providing women with a Gaelic sport of their own. The rules were based on hurling, but modified, with no physical contact permitted. Camogie (*camógaíocht* in Gaelic) was formally established in 1904 with two Dublin clubs meeting in the first game organised under the auspices of the GAA. Cumann Camógaíochta na nGael is now the game's governing body, although this independent Camogie Association remains a part of the GAA family. Its aims and objectives were deemed to be: 'the promotion of Gaelic games and pastimes, the fostering of an awareness of the richness of our national culture and a commitment to the development of a community spirit among the people of all Ireland'.

The game slowly grew in popularity after that first public match in 1904, with more clubs being formed and the game spreading to more counties. The first inter-county game took place in 1912 when Dublin defeated Louth at Jones's Road, which would later become Croke Park. In 1932 the first All-Ireland championship was held, and if the final wasn't staged until 1933, at least a proud competitive dimension had been brought into the game.

Camogie is popular in Ireland today, the game being played in every county. Presently eight of those counties are represented in the senior All-Ireland championship, which is played on an open-draw basis (as opposed to the provincial system), and the final of which takes place in Croke Park. There are also All-Ireland championships at junior and minor level, while the second inter-county competition, the national league, is played at senior and junior level. Clubs meanwhile compete at county, provincial and All-Ireland level. There are also a wide range of colleges and schools competitions.

The Camogie Association follows the same democratic route as the other GAA bodies, with members elected to positions of influence within clubs, County Boards and Provincial Councils. 'Ardchomhairle' is the Gaelic name given to the supreme governing body of the Association, with Ardchomhairle members making their decisions at the annual Congress.

Camogie teams are twelve-a-side, comprising a goal-keeper, four outfield defenders, three centrefield players and four forwards. A camogie pitch can be from 95 to 110 metres in length and from 60 to 80 metres wide. The goals at either end of the pitch are situated in the centre of the respective end-lines. The goal has two goalposts which are 6 metres in height, 4.5 metres apart and joined by a crossbar 2 metres up.

There are two forms of scoring, goals and points, as in football and hurling. Goals are awarded when the ball passes between the goalposts and under the crossbar, and points when the ball passes over the crossbar and between the posts. The small ball (or *sliotar*) is 21 centimetres in diameter and is struck by the camogie stick, known as a *camán*. The *camán* is about three feet in length and three inches in width except for the curved end (the *bas*) which cannot exceed 13 centimetres in width.

The game begins with the referee rolling the *sliotar* along the ground between two opposing players in the centre of the pitch. All physical contact – such as shouldering, pushing, holding or charging – is banned. A player may dispossess an opponent by blocking, hooking, tapping from beneath or flicking the opponent's *camán* from the ground with her own.

Players can strike the *sliotar* on the ground or in the air with the *camán*, catch the *sliotar*, balance it on the *camán*, kick it, take three steps while holding it and handpass it. A player cannot, however, pick the *sliotar* up off the ground with the hand.

Each game lasts fifty minutes, except for inter-county, inter-provincial and All-Ireland club championship games, which are extended to seventy minutes.

As with the other GAA codes, there are camogie strongholds, the game being most popular in Cork and Kilkenny. Dublin have won twenty-six All-Ireland senior championships, but eighteen of these were won in the space of nineteen years between 1948 and 1966. Cork have won eighteen, including four in a row in the 1970s, and Kilkenny's twelve titles include all seven between 1985 and 1991, a remarkable modern-day feat.

The greatest camogie player of modern times is Angela Downey, a Kilkenny player who can make a strong claim to be the greatest player ever to hold a camogie stick. Downey, who was born in 1957, has graced the game throughout the 1970s, 1980s and 1990s, inspiring her county team to an astonishing twelve All-Irelands during that period. A prolific scorer, she plays at full-forward. This supremely talented player has made the era her own and is respected throughout Ireland for her mavellous talent and unprecedented achievements over a long and unparalleled career. She is assisted in her annual destruction of the opposition by her sister

Anne, a talented centrefield player who has also represented Ireland in squash. The Downey sisters are the only two players to have featured in all of Kilkenny's triumphs.

LADIES' FOOTBALL

The role of the female sex in the world of Gaelic football was always 'understood' – at least by the men. Women attended the football matches and cheered their menfolk on. Or they stayed at home and made sure the dinner was ready when the men returned. They washed boots and togs and jerseys and listened to fireside tales of great men of days gone by when neighbours rambled to their house at night.

As clubhouses appeared all over the country in the latter half of the twentieth century, the women of Ireland went on a sandwich-making spree. 'Mick O'Connell or Sean Purcell?' said the men to each other. 'Chicken or ham?' said the women. Excluded. Victims of tradition. Outsiders.

Of course the desire for sporting combat and a passion for the joys of football existed in many female hearts, and there were some rebels who happily flouted tradition. Occasionally a girl might get a game amongst the boys at underage level, but – irrespective of her performance – she would invariably gain little more than condescending comments from adults who saw her participation as a mere novelty, and her interest as something that would wear off as the years went by.

Then it began to change. Women began to play the game together, largely for fun at first, their efforts not taken seriously by male counterparts. Then, as teams and clubs slowly formed, a competitive dimension grew. This was more than a matter of little girls conveniently making up the numbers on boys' school teams. Ladies' football took off slowly at first. Jibes were ignored. More and more teams were formed. Tradition could be turned upside-down if you worked hard enough and were prepared to pursue your goals.

The Ladies' Football Association was duly founded, aptly in the same Hayes's Hotel in Thurles where Michael Cusack and his peers established the GAA. The year was 1974, and just four counties – Offaly, Kerry, Galway and Tipperary – were represented at that first meeting, which was not held, suffice to say, in the hotel's billiards room. The Ladies' Gaelic Football Association (known in Gaelic as Cumann Peile Gael na mBan) independently runs the affairs of ladies' football but, like its camogie counterpart, the body is part of the GAA family.

Since that humble beginning, ladies' football has progressed steadily, slowly at first, but impressively in the 1990s. Since 1974 over 25,000 members have joined the Ladies' Football Association. Each county has its own league and championship, with competition as intense as in the male game, even if the ladies' version struggles to gain the same recognition from the public and the media.

At inter-county level, All-Ireland championships are held for the various grades and age groups. As in the men's game, Kerry is the dominant county in ladies' football, while others that have excelled include Waterford and Laois. London and Manchester both field teams in the All-Ireland ladies' championship.

The game was played in Croke Park for the first time in 1986 and now All-Ireland finals are held there every year. The first ladies' All-Ireland was held in 1989 and was won by Kerry, who retained their title the following season. All-Ireland championships at other levels – including minor (under-18), junior and under-16 – are held. There are also national leagues at senior and junior level.

Over the years the game has grown in popularity in terms

of the numbers playing, and is considered by many to be a better game than the men's version, which is currently beset by too much fouling. The rules of ladies' football are almost exactly the same as those which apply to men's. Physical contact, such as shouldering, is not permitted, however, in the interests of protecting players of lighter physique. When tackling an opponent a player must try to gain possession only by blocking when the other player attempts to kick the ball, or by getting a hand to it as the opponent hops or 'solos' the ball.

The absence of physical exchanges has led to a game which is often much faster and more free-flowing than the men's version. Ladies' football, through its ban on physical contact, is largely free of pulling and dragging (which would be immediately penalised by the referee) and therefore also blissfully unhindered by constant stoppages and inter-ruptions in promising passages of play.

It begs an obvious question: should the male version of Gaelic football outlaw physical contact? On the one hand, it would almost instantly overcome the problems posed by the current absence of an identifiable tackle, reduce instances of rough play and speed up the game, improving it as a spectacle. The alternative view is that taking the physical exchanges out of Gaelic football would rob the game of a large part of its appeal, reducing it to something akin to basketball. No doubt traditionalists would decry such a new-look Gaelic football as being 'a game for ladies' – which of course is what it would be if it followed the path taken by the ladies.

Attempts are being made to raise the profile of ladies' football, with many people, men and women, working tire-lessly to enhance public awareness of the quality of the football and the attractiveness of many of the championships.

Television coverage of the ladies' game has increased and the Croke Park finals, a fitting opportunity for ladies to experience what it is like to play on the famous turf, are enjoyed by thousands of spectators from the participating counties.

The reality, however, is that the game, as with many sports played by both sexes, will always struggle to gain the same profile as the male version. There are far fewer women than men playing Gaelic football, and there is nothing like as much public interest in the women's game. There are obvious reasons for this: the GAA is still overwhelmingly male-dominated, rivalries between men's teams are a century old and it is still the case that considerably more men than women watch sport.

Nonetheless, the trends are moving in the right direction – with more women getting involved, standards improving, and more men showing an interest. Most ladies' teams are coached by men and most games are refereed by men. The same is true of camogie, with many male administrators, coaches and referees. A county final win by a ladies' football club or an All-Ireland victory by a county is greeted with wild celebrations in the given area, and the more success a region experiences the firmer the roots of ladies' football will become.

On the playing front, the ladies of Ireland have rebelled against tradition and done so with consummate style, standing resolutely in the face of initial apathy. The game may still be very much a poor relation, in terms of public and media interest, of the men's game, but it is frequently found to be no such poor relation if analysed from the perspective of quality. Everything points to a game that will prosper further in the future. For it to do so, however, the GAA will have to market it in a more serious way, thus attracting more and more girls to the game.

The GAA should also acknowledge the outstanding con-tribution women can make to the administration of its affairs, and more female members should be enticed to become more actively involved in the running of the Associa-tion. The once token tea-makers became secretaries and public relations officers quite a few years ago and there is no reason why women cannot rise further in the future. The continued increase in the involvement of women in the GAA – on and off the field – can only enhance the Association and bodes well for the continued sporting, social and cultural development of the country.

7

THE PARISH ROOTS OF THE GAA

There are ten minutes to go in the local 'derby' game. Two parishes that would bond together if a local child's pet went missing are kicking the living daylights out of each other on the football pitch. There's a few hundred people at the game on a cold Sunday. The only ones oblivious to what's at stake are the teenage girls who walk around the pitch and the little children at play, the tumbling toddlers who will one day stick out their chests and wear the parish colours with pride.

Men who work side by side in the local factory are jostling, pushing, employing the tricks of the trade, desperate for space and a lucky break, as the referee strives to keep an eye on every off-the-ball incident and his watch imperiously ticks onwards. The play is from end to end, the crowd roaring, lifted now by the passion generated by the impending arrival of the full-time whistle. There are only a couple of points separating the teams and tired legs have received new messages from brains that know the price of failure in a parish derby game.

On the sideline, the managers and their selectors are feeling the pressure. They can hear the critics in the stand, the damning voices easily carrying in the cold stillness. The manager or selector will have a clenched fist, will feel the need to roam along the side of (and frequently on to) the pitch, and will often be armed with an irrational view of all that is unfolding before his eyes. Gaelic football or hurling managers are not unique in this respect, it should be conceded.

With five minutes to go, a controversial free (they're all controversial) is awarded and mayhem ensues. The manager spins around in disgust and looks at his selector, who, wisely, has allowed his face to assume an astonished expression. Substitutes are amazed that the referee should have considered their full-back's hauling of his opponent to the ground as an offence, while in the stand, the precise family background of the official is debated with some vigour.

Suddenly a private boxing bout has begun on another part of the field, with four players exchanging half-hearted punches. Two selectors and the man who carries the water race on to the field and wrestle agonisingly in their minds over whether or not they should join in, or in fact try to stop the proceedings. The referee finally restores order and the free-kick is taken. After the score that results, the manager turns to a nearby substitute and says, 'Sure, how could you win with a referee like that?' It is important for him to cultivate an anti-referee mood, given that his own position could be in jeopardy in the event of his side losing.

As the minutes tick by, a wide spectrum of emotions is experienced by all associated with the losing team. The sense of failure is very real. This was the big one. At times like this the parish is king, the county team an irrelevance. The final whistle sounds and there are handshakes. The games don't always involve outbreaks of wrestling or tough challenges, but in encounters between rival neighbouring parishes, extra 'bite' is often a factor.

It should be said that the referee occasionally remains a

decent man in the eyes of both sides. Sometimes, however, matters can get out of hand and the referee might be gently placed by supporters into the boot of a nearby car, as happened some years ago in an extreme example of fans 'taking issue' with an official's performance.

At the end of the game the handshakes (in most cases) are genuine, and the amateur stars – team-mates and opponents – who will work together tomorrow and who have sweated together today, proceed, invariably, to drink together tonight.

This parish rivalry, as strong between the weakest teams from the smallest parishes as it is between major clubs in bigger areas, is a fundamental strength of the Gaelic Athletic Association. The rivalry is a reflection of just how much the games mean to the people of Ireland, and evidence of the firmness of the GAA's roots in every single parish in the country. These firm roots – the parish structure – are the single most impressive aspect of the GAA, and the envy of all other sports.

The great parish network, which stretches across the whole country and takes in a large percentage of the population at varying levels, is inspired by the GAA's proud tradition and a sense of loyalty to the Association's values, as put in place by its founders and cherished by succeeding generations. It is manifested in many ways. Every parish in Ireland can claim at least one of the 2,700 clubs in existence in the country. Almost all of those clubs have their own grounds (a tiny minority share with neighbouring clubs) and a great many have beautiful clubhouses and other amenities. Many have a number of teams, ensuring that kids as young as seven or eight years of age and middle-aged players alike get a chance to play.

Although the GAA is strong at grassroots level in major

Irish cities, the value and importance of its parish structure is easier to appreciate in rural parts of the country, where it is strongest. In a typical such area, established parish landmarks all show signs of the influence of the Association. Each school will have a GAA field and a number of teams. The local pub will have trophies and photographs of great players from the past on display, not to mention customers with caps, pipes and stories of great feats to tell. The church will have a priest who, whether he likes it or not, will be the club president, a pulpit from which dates of forthcoming games will be announced and a back wall against which men can lean as they reflect during Mass on the local team's chances later that day.

The GAA built this unparalleled foundation largely because it had no real opposition in the early days; those sports that purported to be better alternatives were cast aside by a people delighted that their native games were forging a new identity, and quickly smitten by the competitive edge that developed between local teams following the formation of the GAA. Thus the parish rivalry has been handed down from generation to generation.

That the rivalry was strong in 1884 should not surprise us. The people had few social or sporting outlets. They loved music, song and storytelling, and gathered at night to express that love, but there is a limit to the amount of dancing and singing you can do. The weekends brought football and hurling and athletics, and the sense of competition that has been coveted ever since. When a team lined out for a parish, everyone from the area felt every tackle and every thud of the ball. It became absolutely central to the lives of the people.

Throughout the decades, the parish network grew, the fortunes between neighbouring teams ebbed and flowed, and great rivalries were established. 'Your father played against my father and their fathers played against each other.' 'We beat ye in '46 and we'll beat ye again.' 'Ye never could play the game clean and ye never will.' 'A good man never came out of your parish and if he did ye wouldn't know him.' All good fun.

This hold that the Gaelic Athletic Association has had on the Irish people still looks secure, the rise in popularity of soccer notwithstanding. In soccer games in rural Ireland you are defending your goal; in Gaelic, you are defending the honour of the parish. These days youngsters play soccer and other sports as well as Gaelic games, whereas in the past, either the Ban (on 'foreign' games) was in force or, in post-Ban days, soccer was in some cases still frowned upon.

The GAA net does not miss many players, however. The Association informs the young person of its existence at a very early stage in the child's development. The midwife doesn't quite read you the rules of the Association at birth but the new-born child will only have a few years' freedom before becoming conscious of the presence of the shadow of the GAA.

That shadow hovers over every household, every community centre, every pub and every field, each of the latter a prospective venue for the 'kick-around' in which dreams of stardom are indulged by people who know they will almost certainly never be stars. Then, of course, there are the schools, a foundation for great GAA careers and a vital link in keeping the organisation strong and maintaining the formidable parish structure.

On your way to school, in rural Ireland at least, a football is a vital companion, as my memory can confirm. You might forget your lunch or even your schoolbag, but as you left the house to partake in another of the dubiously labelled 'best days of your life' you were unlikely to forget a ball if one was lying around. The prospect of playing football at school was exciting, but not sufficient. Bringing a ball on the walk to school made that walk less tiresome and you could always imagine that you were a great star. With my school-friends it was Dermot Earley, the celebrated Roscommon player, that we all 'were'.

Many years on, whatever dialogue might have taken place on those walks is lost forever to the memory; the ball and the dreams it created remain in the mind, however. Day-dreaming boys, temporary Dermot Earleys, scored wonderful goals against imaginary goalkeepers in front of thousands of cheering fans and a handful of startled cows. Sometimes a frail boy would be targeted as a goalkeeper and the bewildered 'volunteer' would brace himself as a lunatic ran towards him – assuming something painfully like the voice of commentator Mícheál O'Hehir singing the praises of Dermot Earley – and both ball and goalkeeper would be dispatched to a nearby field. The scorer then proceeded on a lap of honour as bemused council workers dug the 'goalkeeper' out of the ground.

Gaelic football is thus embedded in the psyche of virtually all young boys at this early age. In hurling areas, hurleys are brought on the walks to school. You bring the game to school, you play it there, you play it in the evenings, and in some cases you hear about it at night. Kids will follow their fathers into the local club teams and further oxygen is thus supplied to the great parish rivalry, the GAA's foundation continuously being reinforced.

The parish games that evolve do not officially have the stature of a regular inter-county match, yet they frequently mean much more to the people of a given area. This is the pride factor at work. Pride in the parish. Pride in your son in the centre of the field, or your sister's son, or your daughter's boyfriend. Or in the fact that you prepared the field or gave a lift in your car to two of the substitutes, one of whom is a son of the man you buy Christmas trees from.

The preparing of the field – lining it, erecting nets and flags – is symbolic of the way in which the GAA involves so many in a typical parish. It would not, for example, be unusual for every member of a family to be involved at some level in their local club. In a typical such situation, the father might be the manager or a team selector, a couple of sons would be key players, a daughter would be a passionate supporter and actively trying to set up a ladies' team, and the mother would have been lumbered a long time ago with the kit-washing duties. If it sounds like the females are in a supporting role, in reality that is the way it has been; but, as we have seen, this is now changing.

Of course the great parish rivalry and the impressive capacity of the Association to retain its popularity would not exist were the GAA's games not embraced by the people as the best sporting option open to them. And whatever their faults may be, the games clearly have a vote of confidence from the people. Furthermore, potential rival sports have been kept at bay thus far because the GAA has established such firm roots, involved so many people, and provided the outlets for sporting endeavour that it does.

And while the GAA's organisational talents are far from flawless, it has reaped the benefits of painstakingly developing pitches and other facilities, thus strengthening its hold on towns and villages, as youngsters are naturally attracted to the better-run sporting bodies.

There are, however, some threats to the parish structures that so benefit the GAA. The population of rural Ireland is dwindling, and if this is allowed to continue, it is certain to have an adverse effect on the GAA, reducing the numbers of prospective new players available to the Association. Families are smaller, emigration is a factor and lack of employment forces many young people to travel to bigger towns and cities to find work. Players who leave their parish to work elsewhere will often join a local club in their adopted home. This is happening increasingly, and some have suggested that the pride in the parish may not be as strong as it always was. Some clubs have struggled to field teams. Another worry for the GAA is the continued growth in popularity of soccer, with young children very commonly seen wearing the jerseys of top soccer clubs.

That said, the Association remains relatively strong, its role in Irish society enormous, its hold on the people still formidable. At grassroots level, whole families, notwithstanding their interest and participation in other sports, remain devoted to the the GAA. It remains a prime topic of conversation in the back of the church and in every part of the pub. Our schoolchildren continue to bring footballs and hurleys on their walks to school, even if they may do so in smaller numbers than in the past and despite the fact that a few dreams of Wembley have undoubtedly emerged.

Otherwise sane men unfortunate enough to devote their non-playing days to management continue to develop what can only be described as ferocious tempers, and in some cases complex murder plots, as referees – allegedly – sabotage their clubs' championships hopes. Should we detest such managers? On the contrary, each such man, irrational or otherwise, is the very heart and soul of the GAA and the reason it has thrived. As long as the words 'How would you win with a referee like that?' are uttered, the Gaelic Athletic Association's foundations should be safe and its future secure.

8

GREAT FOOTBALL TEAMS, PLAYERS AND GAMES

Absolutely nothing dominates conversation in Ireland quite like debate about Gaelic games. Soap operas, politicians, the clergy, sex, and other sports all get their verbal airing – but not until a sex scandal in a soap opera involving a sporty priest and a politician comes along will the GAA be threatened as the main topic of conversation in our pubs and homes.

After the mandatory reference to the weather, that other great conversation piece, the talk frequently turns to the great players and teams that have played Gaelic football and hurling, and to the great matches in which they have been involved. More often than not these conversations take place in public houses, where great deeds of old are recalled with wistful wonder. In its own way, it can be as satisfying as actually watching a great game to sit around an open fire and listen or contribute to tales of the men who have raised our native games to such great heights over the years.

Sometimes these public house debates about the all-time greats can lead to impassioned arguments. In these instances no punches will be pulled – in fact, in days gone by, one or two might have been thrown!

GREAT TEAMS

The general consensus, rare to achieve in debates about sporting greatness, is that the greatest team ever to play Gaelic football was the Kerry side that won eight All-Ireland titles between 1975 and 1986. It is widely accepted that this team played Gaelic football to a standard never attained before or since. They were involved in a classic series of matches with another of the game's greatest ever teams, the Dublin side of the mid-1970s. However, before concentrating on those two remarkable teams and their rivalry, there are many others to reflect on who have graced the game since the foundation of the GAA.

In the very early days, Dublin won three All-Irelands in a row (1897–99), and returned to take the titles of 1901 and 1902. Another Dublin three-in-a-row was achieved from 1906 to 1908. Of course very little is known about these teams, and there would have been less competition then than in the years that followed. Perhaps the first really great team of the twentieth century was the Wexford side that won four All-Irelands in a row from 1915 to 1918. This four-in-a-row feat was never surpassed, and was matched only by two different Kerry teams (1929–32 and 1978–81).

Dublin won another three-in-a-row from 1921 to 1923, while a team very highly rated by those who saw it was the Kildare side that won the All-Irelands of 1927 and 1928. Then came the first four-in-a-row Kerry team (1929–32) which peaked with a 3-11 to 0-2 victory over Monaghan in 1930. Kerry added a three-in-a-row from 1939 to 1941, before the first great team from the west of Ireland emerged.

It is rare for Connacht teams to dominate the game (this is partly explained by high emigration levels in the west of Ireland), but over the years the province has produced some of Gaelic football's most stylish teams. The best from the west in the 1940s was the Roscommon team that won the All-Irelands of 1943 and 1944, and was unluckily denied a third in 1946 after a replay with Kerry. The formidable team was led by Jimmy Murray and included stars such as Bill Carlos and Donal Keenan.

The 1940s also saw the emergence of a great Cavan team. Cavan is one of the great GAA counties, with a wonderful footballing tradition and a long history of success. In the early part of the twentieth century Cavan enjoyed a period of dominance within their own province, which was a record of regional superiority unmatched anywhere else in the country. During this extraordinary reign Cavan won twenty-six titles in Ulster in the space of thirty-two years (1918–49). Furthermore, the team that brought All-Ireland glory to the county in 1947 and 1948 can claim to be amongst the greatest of all time. It was a team comprising some of the great names in the game: players such as John Joe O'Reilly, Phil 'The Gunner' Brady, Mick Higgins and Tony Tighe. Cavan also won the All-Ireland of 1952, with some changes in personnel from the 1947–48 side. The county had previously won All-Irelands in 1933 and 1935.

Mayo meanwhile won the All-Irelands of 1950 and 1951 with a fondly remembered team led by the great Sean Flanagan. The 1950s also saw the rise to prominence of a great Galway team which, despite its artistry, was rewarded with just one All-Ireland, in 1956. This team included the so-called 'terrible twins', Frankie Stockwell and Sean Purcell, two all-time greats of the game. In the 1950s Dublin produced a very talented team led by Kevin Heffernan, a player who would later manage the wonderful Dublin team of the 1970s. They won the 1958 All-Ireland, having been defeated in the 1955 decider.

Acknowledged as the greatest team ever to emerge from

the North was the Down side that won successive All-Irelands in 1960 and 1961, playing an exciting style of football and ensuring that they too are ranked amongst history's finest. Their success in 1960 was historic as it was the first time the Sam Maguire Cup went north of the border. Down featured stars such as Sean O'Neill, Joe Lennon, Paddy Doherty and brothers James and Dan McCartan.

Galway atoned for the perceived under-achievement of the 'terrible twins' side by winning three All-Irelands in a row in the 1960s. The team that claimed the titles of 1964, 1965 and 1966 was laden with great stars. Amongst the most famous players were John and Pat Donnellan, Bosco McDermott, Jimmy Duggan and Mattie McDonagh, the only Connacht player to win four All-Ireland football medals. The team's captain, Enda Colleran, later went on to make a career as a GAA TV analyst.

Kerry enjoyed successive All-Ireland wins in 1969 and 1970 and Offaly in 1971 and 1972, although neither was hailed as a particularly special team. What was special was what was to follow. The golden Dublin-Kerry era, which began in the mid-1970s, almost certainly produced the greatest team of all, and arguably the second greatest. Kerry won eight All-Irelands between 1975 and 1986 and Dublin won three between 1974 and 1977, with the teams meeting in several big matches. Mick O'Dwyer (Kerry) and Kevin Heffernan (Dublin) were the managers responsible for assembling these remarkable squads.

First showing their potential when winning the 1975 All-Ireland final, Kerry achieved greatness and underlined their superiority over the rest by winning the finals of 1978, 1979, 1980 and 1981. What would have guaranteed O'Dwyer's team the statistical right to be deemed the greatest of all time was cruelly denied them. In 1982 they were on the verge of winning a fifth consecutive All-Ireland championship (a feat never achieved by any team) when Seamus Darby of Offaly scored a dramatic late goal to deny Kerry that coveted place in history. A number of the team were however still playing when Kerry added three more All-Irelands, while still managed by O'Dwyer, in 1984, 1985 and 1986.

Kevin Heffernan's Dublin defeated the greatest team of all time on a couple of memorable occasions, and of course claimed three All-Irelands for themselves. The Dublin team of that period must ultimately bow to their great rivals, but they did have their moments against Kerry, and they can relish their standing as one of the greatest teams of all time; but they must rue the fact that they were destined to emerge in the same era as the Kerry greats. That Dublin team included gifted and influential players such as Brian Mullins, Tony Hanahoe, Kevin Moran and Jimmy Keaveney.

GREAT PLAYERS

The debate over who is the greatest player in the history of Gaelic football will run for as long as the game is played – and for as long as fans sit around open fires. Naturally, given that county's rate of success, Kerry players figure prominently in any discussion about greats. One of these is the man frequently referred to as the greatest centrefield player of all time – Mick O'Connell.

O'Connell had everything a footballer could wish for. Of perfect physique for the game, he had strength, pace and a sharp football brain. A highly accomplished free-taker, a great passer, and blessed with a mastery of just about every skill a player needed, it was his majestic fielding that was most responsible for making him a folk hero. He played the game in the 1950s, 1960s and early 1970s and did so with great distinction, gaining a deserved reputation for sportsmanship as well as supreme ability. An unassuming sporting giant who lived on Valentia Island, he played the game for the love of it and saw victory as virtually a secondary consideration. When it was all over on each big match day, as thousands regaled thousands more with tales of O'Connell's latest feats, he returned by boat, no doubt shrugging his shoulders, to the peace and quiet of his island life.

Other great Kerry players over the years include Paddy Bawn Brosnan, Mick O'Dwyer – an accomplished star before becoming a legendary manager – Jack O'Shea, Pat Spillane and Mike Sheehy, the last three being members of the all-conquering teams of the 1970s and 1980s.

O'Shea was a wonderfully versatile player. Although he made his name as a high-fielding midfielder, in the latter part of his career he played in various other positions, using his experience, stamina and all-round skills to great effect.

Magnificent to watch in full flow, Spillane was one of the most exciting players in the game's history, who mesmerised fans with his thrilling solo runs and superb scores. He was, quite simply, a master of the game, at times appearing to be bonded to the ball as he raced across his playground, Croke Park, making magic and leaving opponents trailing in his wake. He has since proved he is human by becoming a controversial television analyst and newspaper columnist.

Sheehy was one of the greatest opportunists of all time, a brilliant score-taker who graced Croke Park with many memorable performances. His superb scores and astute link-up play were highlights of his game.

Throughout the decades there have been countless men who have thrilled fans with their feats and become heroes. John Joe O'Reilly was a Cavan legend in the 1940s while Sean Purcell of Galway will always figure in any debate about Gaelic football greats. Purcell starred on the Galway team that won the 1956 All-Ireland and was a remarkably versatile player with a mastery of all Gaelic football's skills. There are many who would say that he was the all-time king of the game.

MODERN-DAY GREATS

In the 1970s and early 1980s, Matt Connor of Offaly, whose glorious career was sadly cut short by a car accident, was recognised as an attacking genius. Modern-day greats who would rank with the best include Colm O'Rourke, a distinguished and long-serving forward with Meath, and Kerry's Maurice Fitzgerald, presently the outstanding footballer in the game.

Fitzgerald's performance in the 1997 All-Ireland final against Mayo ranks as one of the greatest ever individual displays by a player. Without Fitzgerald in such form, Kerry would not have won. He graced that final, scoring from every conceivable area of Croke Park, the dressing-rooms apart. Peter Canavan of Tyrone, a present-day star, and Larry Tompkins of Cork, who starred in the 1980s and early 1990s, are both greatly revered for their playing exploits.

Of course a tendency when discussing greats is to opt for attacking players, the stars whose scores have brought you to your feet. Defenders should not be overlooked, however – they are just as worthy of celebration as flashy forwards! A king of defenders whose mastery of his role will always be remembered was Paidi O'Shea of Kerry, who played in the 1970s and 1980s.

There are many, many more players in all positions, from all counties, who have graced the game with distinction and who are capable of earning a barman's frown as the fireside debate about all-time greats enters the late hours. Indeed, many who played for unsuccessful counties, often having just one outing in the championship in a year, possessed the genius we so regularly saw in players who gained greater exposure.

MEMORABLE GAMES

The ultimate sporting fantasy for a spectator is to witness two all-time giants of a particular sport do battle against one another. Because they are so rare, such instances are cherished. Tennis fans were fortunate enough to witness a number of great games between Bjorn Borg and John McEnroe in the 1970s and 1980s. Of course, they would have liked to have seen either man play Rod Laver, an all-time tennis great from a previous era. The brilliant young American golfer Tiger Woods is tipped by some to become the greatest ever, but how we would have loved to have seen him in a head-to-head with Jack Nicklaus when the 'Golden Bear' was at his peak. To see Muhammad Ali in action against great heavyweights of different eras, like Rocky Marciano or Mike Tyson, would have resolved some arguments and provided magical entertainment.

Just occasionally history is kind enough to deliver all-time greats in the one era – as in the case of McEnroe and Borg – and the result, for the public, is a sample of sporting heaven. It happened in Gaelic football in the 1970s, when two truly great teams met in a series of major championship matches before an enthralled public. At least two of those meetings between Kerry and Dublin deserve to rank amongst the great games in history.

In 1977 the two super-sides met in a memorable All-Ireland semi-final. Dublin were champions, having defeated Kerry in the previous year's final. In doing so, they had gained revenge for Kerry's win over them in the 1975 showpiece.

The next showdown between the teams was therefore

looked forward to with keen anticipation by fans across Ireland. Almost 55,000 were in Croke Park for the match, which produced some wonderful passages of football, beautiful tapestries being woven by masters of their art. As with most great games, there was drama. Dublin were leading for the first time in the game, with just fourteen minutes remaining. Nobody was making tea in the households of Ireland.

Kerry responded and led by two points (1-13 to 1-11) with six minutes left. Suddenly Dublin pounced with two great goals. They added a late point and at the final whistle had won a classic encounter by 3-12 to 1-13 with a scintillating final flourish that befitted a splendid occasion. Dublin duly went on to win the final against Armagh.

The golden era continued in 1978 when Kerry and Dublin again emerged from the pack and met in that year's All-Ireland final. The game turned out to be remarkably one-sided but was so action-packed and dramatic that it too deserves recognition as one of the great Gaelic football occasions.

Dublin, the champions, made a brilliant start and led by five points after just twenty minutes. Their supremacy over Kerry looked likely to continue. But the next fifteen minutes were to prove defining moments in the history of Kerry football and in the rivalry of these two great teams. Kerry scored three quick goals, the first completely against the run of play, the second, by Mike Sheehy, a famous effort which saw the genial Kerryman take a quick free-kick, guiding an imaginative and beautifully judged lob into an empty net when the Dublin goalkeeper Paddy Cullen was off his line remonstrating with the referee over the initial decision. The goal will stand as a sublime reminder of an artist in his heyday.

The peerless Con Houlihan, writing in the *Evening Press*,

described the drama as only he could: ' . . . Mike Sheehy was running up to take the kick, and suddenly Paddy dashed back toward his goal like a woman who smells a cake burning. The ball won the race and it curled inside the near post as Paddy crashed into the outside of the net and lay against it like a fireman who had returned to find his station ablaze.' Dublin were shattered by the transformation and a rampant Kerry went on to win a most unusual and memorable match by a seventeen-point margin (5-11 to 0-9).

Kerry added the All-Irelands of 1979, 1980 and 1981, but the 1982 All-Ireland title, which they required for a record-breaking five-in-a-row, was to elude them. That final did not produce quality football throughout, but its finale was so dramatic – and the consequences of that late drama so great – that the game is certain to gain prominence in the pages of footballing history.

Offaly had been decisively beaten by Kerry in the previous year's final and few expected them to prevent Kerry from winning again, including the doomed entrepreneur who was busy producing commemorative five-in-a-row merchandise.

Kerry were four points in front as the game entered the final six minutes, their fans preparing to celebrate a historic milestone. Destiny, however, had other plans.

Offaly firstly reduced Kerry's lead by scoring two points, and then pounced with a dramatic winning goal in the dying seconds. Seamus Darby's score was controversial, with the player accused of pushing an opponent before fielding the ball. However, the goal would win an All-Ireland and deny Kerry their place in history – and our entrepreneurial friend his anticipated profits. Arguments still rage about the alleged push, but historians are not interested. The Sam Maguire Cup had gone to Offaly and Kerry were left without the final piece of evidence needed to convince the few remaining doubters that they truly were the greatest team ever to play the game.

In the 1940s, Roscommon, Kerry and Cavan were involved in some memorable matches. The Roscommon team that won the All-Irelands of 1943 and 1944 (defeating Kerry and Cavan) were denied a third title in 1946 after a most dramatic game against Kerry.

Roscommon were comfortably ahead in the final minutes. Legend has it that Jimmy Murray, who had captained them to their great successes in 1943 and 1944, was formulating his acceptance speech as he received treatment for an injury on the sideline. The sporting gods cherish their powers, however, and periodically remind us that they are lovers of drama. Cue two late Kerry goals, a shock draw, and a Kerry win in the replay. Jimmy Murray's words were never uttered, the Sam Maguire Cup once again torn between two lovers.

Kerry and Cavan met in unusual circumstances in 1947, when for the first time ever the All-Ireland final was played outside Ireland, the Polo Grounds in New York being the venue. Of course the Irish took over the Polo Grounds, while Cavan took home the Sam Maguire Cup. Back in Ireland, just about everyone listened in wonder to the words of Mícheál O'Hehir, whose commentary on the game would itself go into folklore.

One of the great games of the 1950s was the 1956 All-Ireland final in which Frankie Stockwell, one of the great figures in the history of the GAA, scored a superb two goals and five points to ensure that his Galway team defeated Cork.

Undoubtedly one of the greatest games ever to be played was the 1970 Leinster final which featured a team that scored five goals and at one stage led by eleven points – and still lost! Meath and Offaly were the contestants, with Meath winning an incredible game by 2-22 to 5-12. In later years new Meath teams would show similarly amazing fighting qualities and the county's footballers are now suspected of being descendants of Lazarus.

Kerry and Cork, the two premier teams in the province, have contested some tremendous Munster finals throughout the years and few could equal what happened in 1976. The first game ended in a draw, with the replay producing a classic, and a second draw, Kerry 3-13, Cork 2-16. Munster final day, invariably a colourful extravaganza and a majestic celebration of the uniqueness of Gaelic games, had rarely been so exciting. Cork were sunk in the second replay.

In 1983 the All-Ireland final was no classic in terms of the quality of football, but it will always be remembered. Dublin had three men sent off, while opponents Galway lost one. At times you could almost feel the intensity from your living-room armchair, where you were just about safe. The final became notorious, although the players involved insist they got a bad press, and probably didn't enter the referee in any 'Man of the Year' awards either. At the close of battle, the cruelly labelled 'dirty dozen' of Dublin had held on for a famous backs-to-the-wall victory by 1-10 to 1-8.

The following year the Ulster final produced one of the greatest individual performances in history when Tyrone full-forward Frank McGuigan scored eleven points from general play (no free-kicks) in his team's 0-15 to 1-7 win over Armagh. Later that year a car crash tragically cut short McGuigan's career. He has a coveted place in the GAA history books, however, and video reruns of his wonderful lofted points on that magical afternoon are a pleasure to watch again and again.

Throughout the late 1980s and early 1990s Dublin and Meath established a rivalry in Leinster that kept the public riveted. The Meath-Dublin games were fiercely competitive, with intense physical exchanges often spilling over into violence. However, the two teams' many great tussles also produced spells of superb football. The greatest example of how well matched the Dublin and Meath teams were came in 1991 when the counties were involved in the most re-markable championship tie in the history of the GAA. That first-round Leinster championship meeting took an amazing four games before a winner emerged. There has never been anything quite like it before or since. It was as if the footballing gods were declaring to the world that they could not separate the two. After three draws (two of which involved extra-time) the decisive game took place on 6 July, and maintained the drama to the end.

Dublin led by six points with fifteen minutes remaining, and the 61,000 privileged to be inside Croke Park were convinced that the saga was about to end in Dublin's favour. Meath, managed by Sean Boylan, were famous for their fighting qualities and never-say-die approach, attributes already witnessed in abundance in the previous three games, and during their All-Ireland successes in 1987 and 1988. However, the task ahead of them now seemed immense.

Meath clawed back to within three points of Dublin, and then, in the final minute, in a slick handpassing move that the great Dublin team of the 1970s would have been proud of, they produced a memorable goal from defender Kevin Foley. Moments later they added the winning point. Croke Park had never seen anything like it and the greatest saga in the game's history had ended in fittingly sensational fashion.

In 1997 Kildare and Meath had to meet three times to decide their Leinster championship tie after the first two games ended level. Both were footballing classics, featuring superb, open and entertaining play. Meath finally emerged victorious.

This is just a flavour of some of the most fondly remembered games of the past sixty years or so. There have
been many others over the years that live in the memory, but
sadly we cannot mention all of them here. These are games
that have risen above mediocrity and negativity, making
ordinary summer Sundays become scorching hot days in the
mind. The great games are thrilling battles that have crowds
gasping during the action, and buzzing at the end, as they
leave whatever theatre of dreams has played host to the day's
drama.

9

GREAT HURLING TEAMS, PLAYERS AND GAMES

If the Kerry team of the 1970s and 1980s is accepted by most fans as the greatest Gaelic football side of all time, the hurling equivalent is not so easily agreed upon. Of course, the issue is quickly resolved in Kilkenny, Cork and Tipperary, where the natives of each county would happily plump for a team from within their own revered ranks.

Cork won four All-Irelands in a row between 1941 and 1944, while three-in-a-row winners in history include Cork (1892–94, 1952–54 and 1976–78), Tipperary (1898–1900) and Kilkenny (1911–13). These were all great teams by virtue of their achievements, but who is to say that any one of them was history's greatest? Apart from the arduous task of trying to compare teams of different eras, one has to take into account that with more and more counties now a force in hurling, teams that have won even one All-Ireland (and certainly two) in the current competitive era may well be reaching a standard of excellence comparable with anything that has been attained before.

As to speculation on which was the greatest hurling team of them all, many neutrals would deem it to be the Cork team of the mid-1970s, but a case could also be made for the Tipperary team of the early and mid-1960s or the Kilkenny team of the early 1970s. There have been several other great teams, however, and it is best to celebrate them all and let the arguments rage!

Looking back over the twentieth century, numerous teams appear worthy of special mention. Tipperary won three All-Irelands in a row at the turn of the century (1898–1900), matching Cork's similar achievement a few years earlier (1892–94). Kilkenny enjoyed a three-in-a-row from 1911 to 1913, and produced one of the great sides of the first half of the century two decades later. That team won the All-Irelands of 1932, 1933 and 1935.

The Limerick team that won All-Irelands in 1934 and 1936 (and lost the finals of 1933 and 1935) would be considered amongst history's finest by those who saw them in action. If one is to go by statistics (not necessarily the right approach, as great teams can also be unlucky ones) the Cork side that won four All-Irelands between 1941 and 1944 can lay claim to being history's greatest. No other team has won four consecutive All-Ireland senior hurling titles, and it is difficult to imagine any side ever doing so again, especially at a time when more and more powers are emerging. That Cork team was inspired by Jack Lynch, one of the great names of hurling, who went on to become Taoiseach (Prime Minister) of Ireland.

Tipperary won three successive All-Irelands in 1949, 1950 and 1951 and would be regarded as one of the most accomplished teams ever, while Cork had yet another three-in-a-row from 1952 to 1954. Always spoken of as all-time greats were the Wexford team who won the All-Irelands of 1955 and 1956. That team featured two legends of the game, the Rackard brothers – Bobby and the one and only Nicky.

Tipperary had arguably its best ever team (and perhaps history's) a decade or so later when winning the All-Irelands of 1961, 1962, 1964 and 1965. Furthermore, they were the beaten finalists in 1960, 1967 and 1968. This great team had stars such as Michael 'Babs' Keating (later a successful manager), Theo English, the great Jimmy Doyle, Donie Nealon and John Doyle.

Kilkenny had an exceptional team in the early 1970s, which won the All-Irelands of 1972, 1974 and 1975 and featured masters of the game such as Noel Skehan, Pat Henderson, Frank Cummins and the genial all-time great Eddie Keher. Then came the superb Cork team that won three in a row from 1976 to 1978 and featured one of the greatest players in the history of the game, Jimmy Barry Murphy, who was also an accomplished footballer. Other star players included Ray Cummins, Johnny Crowley and Charlie McCarthy. Remembered with fondness too is the great Kilkenny team that won back-to-back All-Irelands in 1982 and 1983, beating great rivals Cork on both occasions.

Hurling has always had a great tradition in Galway, but apart from an All-Ireland win in 1923 the county was starved of success until a great team came along in the 1980s. Galway won the All-Irelands of 1980, 1987 and 1988 and were finalists in 1981, 1985 and 1986. Amongst the stars from the west was the dashing Gerry McInerney, who looked like he had come from the set of a Mexican gangster movie (he hadn't), but hurled like a man possessed. Other Galway masters of the ash in the 1980s included Peter Finnerty, Tony Keady, Sylvie Linnane and the majestic Joe Cooney.

In the 1990s honours have been spread out amongst a number of powers but there are those who believe (not least in Clare) that the Clare team that won the All-Irelands of 1995 and 1997 would have been a match for any from past eras.

GREAT PLAYERS

Among the greatest hurling players of all time are Mick Mackey (Limerick), Jimmy Doyle (Tipperary), Eddie Keher (Kilkenny), Jack Lynch (Cork), Lory Meagher (Kilkenny), M. J. 'Inky' Flaherty (Galway), Jackie Power (Limerick) and the Rackard brothers, Bobby and Nicky (Wexford). Jimmy Barry Murphy was a Cork superstar in the 1970s while modern-day contenders would include Joe Cooney (Galway), D. J. Carey (Kilkenny), Brian Lohan (Clare) and Nicholas English (Tipperary).

RING THE KING

However, those who were fortunate enough to see him play insist that Cork's Christy Ring was the greatest hurler of all time. To demonstrate how strong a candidate he is for the accolade, it might be sufficient to say that I believe he was the greatest – and I never saw him hold a hurley. I have, however, heard the stories of his feats so often, and from so many sources, that I am conditioned to believe (and have no reason to question it) that Ring was born to be the king of hurlers.

I have no doubt that every man who ever hurled in the thousands of years over which we have played the game would see in Ring a fitting symbol of everything a king of hurling should be. The 'Wizard from Cloyne' scored goals with amazing regularity and was a master of all the great skills of the ancient game. His career spanned an amazing twenty-four years at county level alone and his consistency in producing great performances was remarkable.

Ring was the consummate team player, yet a showman; a battler who enjoyed the physical exchanges but also an artist who took pleasure in exhibiting his dazzling array of skills. If Christy Ring was not the greatest hurler of all time, the question is: who in God's name was? There are some who can be spoken of in the same breath as Ring, but to be adjudged the greatest player of all time, any one of them would have to be deemed to have been superior to him. Case, it would appear, closed.

Due credit has to be accorded to those who could at least compare to Ring. Mackey, the Limerick star of the 1930s and 1940s, certainly could. He was an artist who could make magic with the hurley; a stylist, an entertainer, a swash-buckling hero who brought fans to their feet.

Nicky Rickard was a superb forward, a great score-taker who had strength, skill and indefatigable spirit. Kilkenny's ace Eddie Keher, who played in the 1960s and 1970s, was a genius; he ghosted past opponents and scored seemingly at will.

As with great teams, how does one determine who the greatest players were? We are dealing with different eras, different opponents, different games, different types of game in some cases. The fans around the bar-room fire will never agree; part of the appeal of this debate is the knowledge that it can never really have a definitive conclusion. Suffice to say that Christy Ring is certainly the 'man to beat' in hurling terms, just as many would say that Mick O'Connell was the ultimate prince of Gaelic footballers. Fans of Mick Mackey and Sean Purcell might begin the orderly protests, ac-companied by the shaking of a despondent barman's head.

But as we know, the greatest sportsmen of all time are ultimately our own personal property. It is our hearts that they lift, our expectations they satisfy, our hopes they deliver. My 'greatest of all time' does not have to be yours. Yours may seem a bizarre choice to me, but he's still yours. There will be opinion polls, newspaper articles, television debates, exchanges amongst experts and public-house fire-side chats, but nobody will ever really own the titles that, from time to time, will be bestowed upon them.

Each 'great' knows that time does not stand still and that, as the debates rage, new greats are commanding the *sliotar* in school fields. These are tomorrow's superstars – doctors or lawyers perhaps in their mothers' eyes, but sporting giants in destiny's plan. This is part of the magic of sport. There are Christy Rings, Mick Mackeys and D. J. Careys as yet unborn. We can marvel at the great teams and great heroes of the past – we always should and always will – but we must also look to the future for new stars, new feats and the realisation of new dreams on our sporting fields.

WONDERFUL GAMES

The clash of the ash meanwhile has produced a series of wonderful games in every era and, once again, only a handful can be alluded to here. Over the last half century or so, fans have been thrilled by frequent outstanding battles. Looking back to the 1950s, two memorable games in 1956 stand out. Both involved Wexford. That year's league final was one of the most astonishing games of all time. Opponents Tipperary led the Wexford men by a massive fifteen points (2-10 to 0-1) at half-time. Conditions were stormy on an occasion which would become known as 'the Day of the Big Wind'. Wexford of course had the wind at their backs in the second half, but they had been out-hurled to such an extent and were so far behind that their eventual victory is still astonishing. By the final whistle they had transformed a fifteen-point deficit into a four-point triumph – an amazing win that is a real contender for the comeback of all time.

In the same year's All-Ireland hurling final the play between Wexford and Cork ebbed and flowed in thrilling fashion from the first puck to the final whistle. Wexford were once again the winners, and the game is remembered for a crucial late save by their goalkeeper Art Foley from the great aristocrat, Cork's hurling legend Christy Ring. Having engaged all his strength in trying to do what came natural to him – to crash the *sliotar* into the net – Ring watched Foley's save in amazement, and then continued running goalward as play moved away from the goal. The mission of a sporting legend who had just seen a chance of All-Ireland victory denied? To shake hands with the man who had thwarted him.

The 1957 final was a high-scoring classic in which Kilkenny made a dramatic comeback to defeat Waterford by 4-10 (22) to 3-12 (21). Waterford had led by 3-10 to 2-7 midway through the second half. Kilkenny closed the gap with some inspired scores and during riveting exchanges they got to within one point of the leaders with eight minutes of play left. Sean Clohosey then levelled the scores and a remarkable victory was sealed when Mickey Kelly struck the winning point. There was further drama to come as the *sliotar* was caught by a fan who didn't wish to return it – he must have been from Kilkenny – and the referee was accused of not adding on enough time to compensate for this time-wasting.

In 1959 there was an amazing All-Ireland final between Waterford and Kilkenny, which ended in a draw with a scoreline of Waterford 1-17, Kilkenny 5-5. Waterford won the replay for only their second senior title. The first All-Ireland hurling final to be televised was the 1962 decider in which counties Tipperary and Wexford duly rose to the occasion, Tipperary winning a great match by 3-10 to 2-11.

In 1966 hurling connoisseurs Cork and Kilkenny met in a superb All-Ireland final, won by Cork, 3-9 to 1-10. The 1968 final was another classic and again involved a remarkable comeback. (Such comebacks are more common in hurling than in most other sports as the game produces more scores and the speed at which it is played can lead to swift changes in fortune.) Wexford were trailing by eight points to Tipperary at half-time in that 1968 final but produced a sparkling second-half performance and ensured that the game would live in the memory. By midway into the second half the sides were level (3-6 to 1-12) when a goal by the great Tony Doran put Wexford into the lead. They added a quick point and another goal to go 5-7 to 1-12 in front. A stunned Tipperary still had the resolve to respond with two late goals of their own, leaving them an agonising single point behind. A late chance to equalise was squandered and Wexford emerged victorious in a classic final.

Another classic clash of the ash was the 1972 final in which the protagonists were Kilkenny and Cork. Both sides had been in devastating form in their previous games, Kilkenny defeating Galway by 5-28 to 3-7 and Cork scoring 7-20 against London. The final proved to be an exceptionally high-scoring match which featured sensational passages of hurling before Kilkenny emerged as winners by 3-24 to 5-11.

Two years later (1974) Kilkenny played in another of the era's great games, winning a high-scoring Leinster final against Wexford. The 1975 All-Ireland semi-final, in which Galway beat a Cork team who were destined to win the All-Ireland finals of 1976, 1977 and 1978, was also a classic, as was the 1976 final, when Cork defeated Wexford by 2-21 to 4-11.

Galway's famous victory in 1980, ending a fifty-seven-year famine for the county, came at the expense of Limerick in a memorable game. There were emotional scenes afterwards, as Galway fans celebrated a crucial breakthrough for the county, which had too frequently played a supporting role. The high-scoring 1984 Munster final, which featured an amazing Cork comeback at the expense of Tipperary, is often referred to as one of the great games of the past forty years or so.

The 1987 Munster final between Tipperary and Cork was a wonderful high-scoring draw while the 1987 All-Ireland semi-final saw Galway defeat Tipperary 3-20 to 2-17. It was a thrilling game in which the pace and intensity never relented.

Galway also featured in a classic game in 1990, when the All-Ireland final between the Connacht ambassadors and Cork featured an amazing forty-three scores. Cork claimed just twenty of those scores to Galway's twenty-three but were still deserved winners of a breathtaking encounter by 5-15 to 2-21.

The 1994 final featured a dramatic late transformation when Offaly, out-hurled for an hour or so of the game's seventy minutes and looking certain losers against Limerick, produced a spellbinding five-minute phase of hurling that would have done honour to any team in history. For five minutes their hurleys became wands, and after a series of spectacular scores (2-5), a devastated Limerick saw the Liam McCarthy Cup stolen from their grasp.

These are just some of the hurling games that have thrilled fans and tested sportswriters' vocabularies. There have been many more, and quite a few of them in less auspicious surroundings than Croke Park or the various provincial final venues.

At various levels of the game there have been wonderful exhibitions of athletic prowess, although memorable performances by individuals or teams on big occasions are probably deserving of special commendation. It is the promise of witnessing more glorious feats that brings the fans back and the prospect of achieving them that inspires the hurlers of the towns and villages of Ireland.

10

THE GAA AND POLITICS

Those who say that sport and politics shouldn't mix must shake their heads in despair when they think of the Gaelic Athletic Association. The GAA has always been inextricably linked with politics, something which it must be said it could hardly avoid, given that it was born in, and partly because of, a politically volatile climate.

Not only has the GAA been entrenched in politics since its foundation, it has even been linked with armed resistance by the Irish to British rule. The GAA was suspected of major involvement in the historic 1916 Rising and the turbulent conflict that followed, which led to the partition of Ireland in 1922. The Association has denied any such involvement and insists it is non-political, if still largely committed to the ideal of a united Ireland. However, while denying that it had any role in the Easter Rising or other such militant activity, the GAA would always have accepted that many of its members may have been associated with organisations who were involved.

What cannot be denied is the GAA's distrust of and distaste for the British political establishment. Historically, this animosity towards England has perhaps been most notably demonstrated by the GAA's disapproval of 'rival'

British games. Its refusal to have anything to do with English sport was most famously highlighted by the imposition of a ban on members of the Association playing or attending 'foreign games' such as soccer and rugby. This ban, which was lifted in 1971, was stark evidence of the anti-British thinking that prevailed in the GAA when it was formed and that continued to exist over many subsequent decades.

Although the GAA's political role has lessened greatly over the years, it still has nationalist sympathies and is thus seen by many as a divisive force in Northern Ireland, where six counties have remained under British rule since the partition of Ireland.

The two communities in the North have very different views on the GAA. Republicans and nationalists are, in general terms, committed to the Association and its ideals, and comforted in times of crisis by its presence in the shadows. Most – but not all – unionists and Protestants reject and in some cases detest the GAA because they see it as a strictly nationalist organisation with nothing to offer them. The GAA continues to develop its games on a thirty-two county basis, an ever-present reminder to unionists of where its loyalties lie.

Furthermore, while the GAA's infamous Ban is gone, the Association continues to implement its controversial Rule 21, a second ban which precludes members of the British security forces based in Northern Ireland from playing its games. This is seen by most unionists and Protestants as a sectarian and outdated policy that exposes the GAA as an anti-Protestant and politically motivated body with no interest in extending the hand of friendship to outsiders. The GAA would argue that some of its members have been murdered during the Troubles, simply because they were GAA members, and that the Association is periodically subjected to harassment by the British security forces and others. The occupation of the GAA's Casement Park in Belfast by the British forces is put forward as a stark example of the treatment the GAA has been subjected to, and damage to property there is seen as symbolic of the security forces' harassment of the Association in the North.

To appreciate why the GAA and the political fortunes of Ireland will always be linked, we only have to reflect on its roots and on the political climate which led to its formation.

The anglicisation of Ireland had been ongoing since the imposition of British rule on the Irish. Rule by London was put in place with the passing of the Act of Union in 1800 which, with no regard for the wishes of the Irish people, had ended the existence of Ireland as a political unit and effectively made it a part of the United Kingdom. The famine and its effects drained the people of the energy to concentrate on the fight for political freedom for a period, but the desire to gain independence from England lived on in men's hearts. The Irish Republican Brotherhood (IRB) was founded in 1858 and the new group, which boasted signficant strength and whose members were to become known as the 'Fenians', vowed to fight against British rule. The IRB were to play a role in helping to create the GAA, encouraging Michael Cusack, as we have seen, to take the course of action he eventually did.

With the Land League taking on the landlord system at that time, and with serious unrest in the country, it is clear that the climate among the Irish was one of great resentment at their lack of independence.

Reminders of that lack of independence were visible on the playing fields, where there was weekly evidence of the suppression of native games and the growing influence of outside ones. Athletics meetings were subjected to British rules; rugby and cricket were played all over Ireland, at the behest of the English gentry. Any attempt by the native people to partake in their unique pastimes, such as hurling, was frowned upon. Irish games could not continue to breathe in such a climate. As leading GAA historian Padraig Purcell noted in his book *The GAA in Its Time*:

> ... by the 1880s the tide of anglicisation was flowing so strongly that the future of Irish nationalism was threatened. The rising middle classes were in more danger than others of being led away from the national ideals, since social and material advantages as well as promotional preferment could be gained by attachment to Dublin Castle (then British Headquarters in Ireland) and all that the Castle stood for.

The GAA was duly set up in 1884, with its founders desperate to seize control of Ireland's native games and preserve them from English influence, while also totally committed to the fight for freedom and the winning of independence for the Irish people. For obvious reasons, the Association was welcomed by everyone in the nationalist movement. To succeed in reviving Irish games and gaining independence for them – with the Irish governing their own sports – would have the welcome additional benefit of preserving Irish culture, strengthening the national identity, and lifting the spirits of the people. It would do nothing but good for the fight to gain political freedom. Indeed most early clubs were named after famous Irish patriots.

The GAA soon came under suspicion from the British, who quickly established that at best it would have many staunch republicans as members and at worst would be a 'front' for military groups actively pursuing an anti-British agenda. In response the GAA argued, as it frequently would, that it was not a political organisation, but a national one.

Nonetheless, as a leading member of the nationalist family, it was constantly interlinked with the political developments of the time. The Irish Republican Brotherhood controlled the GAA at one point, and this led to the Catholic Church briefly turning against the Association, labelling it a recruiting ground for the nationalist cause.

In time, the IRB's influence on the GAA would diminish, but the Association continued to be strongly linked to the nationalist cause. It was usual for the GAA to send large numbers of its members to funerals of leading nationalist figures, and often the GAA mourners would carry hurleys, holding them as soldiers would hold rifles.

The GAA's protestations that it was non-political were difficult to take seriously. Its role in the militant resistance to British rule is a constant source of intrigue. Certainly the British were convinced of GAA involvement in the 1916 Rising, the rebellion that led to the War of Independence, which in turn led to the establishment of an independent Irish government in 1922 and the setting up of the border which separates the Republic of Ireland from the six northern counties still under British rule.

THE 1916 RISING

The belief that the GAA was involved in a coordinated way in the Rising may have been paranoia on the part of the British. However, it is accepted that a large number of GAA members took up arms during the short-lived revolution. Again, it is necessary to reflect on the times and the mood that prevailed in the country.

The GAA was among the organisations credited with

leading the cultural revival in Ireland that led indirectly to the revolution of 1916. The spirits of the people had been lifted. A downtrodden race had responded with enthusiasm to the revival of their games, as masterminded by this great national movement. The self-belief thus created led to a surge in national pride, a sense of national identity and a new appetite for fighting British rule.

The recently formed Irish Volunteers, a militant group intent on revolution, undoubtedly attracted many young GAA members into their ranks. When the Rising finally took place, on Easter Monday 1916, it was to last for just a week. The small number involved on the Irish side surrendered, but sixteen of the group's leaders were executed. Two thousand more suspected of involvement, including many leading GAA members, were deported to English jails.

The British allegations of GAA involvement in the Rising were rejected by the Association, which again stated that it was non-political but added that its members were free to join any group or association they wished.

Whatever the extent of its members' role in the Rising, the Association certainly suffered in the aftermath. British police began to disrupt GAA games and for a brief period all such games were banned. A campaign of harassment of GAA personnel followed.

As the Irish public reacted angrily to the executions of the leaders of the Rising, the GAA played an important supportive role for prisoners, firmly nailing its green colours to the mast. It raised large sums of money for 'National Aid', the fundraising drive organised to help Irish Volunteers who were incarcerated in British jails.

The British later sought to introduce conscription in Ireland, their intention being to recruit more troops for the armies still fighting the First World War. The notion was vigorously opposed by all members of Ireland's nationalist family, including the GAA, anti-conscription meetings being held in conjunction with matches. The Association was predictably targeted as punishment for such insolence, with leading members arrested and harassed.

The separate war in which the British police and the GAA were now involved escalated with the GAA's refusal to pay a new 'entertainments tax' applicable to the playing of games. Official permits were now required before games could be played but the GAA organised a mass series of games on 4 August 1918 – billed as 'Gaelic Sunday' – in which an estimated 100,000 people came out and played, without permits, in defiance of British harassment. The harassment ended thereafter.

BLOODY SUNDAY 1920

The war did not end, however. In 1919 the Volunteers (now the IRA) began a concerted campaign against the crown forces and the War of Independence, which would rage for two and a half years, was under way. It would also lead to the blackest day in the history of the GAA, once again implicating the Association in politics and war. As part of the ongoing hostilities, on the morning of 21 November 1920 the Irish Volunteers killed fourteen British spies in various locations in Dublin. The republican side would later claim that the fourteen were plotting the assassination of Sinn Féin leaders. It was a bloody beginning to a dark day.

That afternoon Dublin were playing Tipperary in a challenge game in Croke Park which was being watched by around 10,000 spectators. At about 3 o'clock a group of the dreaded Black and Tans (a notorious irregular British regiment) suddenly appeared at the ground and began to shoot indiscriminately into the crowd. An inevitable stampede resulted, as players and spectators ran for cover. At the end of the turmoil, thirteen lay dead, including the captain of the Tipperary team, Michael Hogan, in whose memory a section of the ground was later named the Hogan Stand.

That the British should have targeted a GAA match to avenge the killings earlier that morning was revealing. It seems unlikely that they selected Croke Park randomly on the basis that a large group of people would be gathered there, and that the attack would cause maximum publicity and enrage the public. All of that was guaranteed; but much more convincing is the view that they linked the GAA with the volatile atmosphere of the time and considered the Association to be firmly allied with the struggle for independence that had grown in popularity since 1916. The fateful episode became known as 'Bloody Sunday' and naturally only hardened the hostile attitude towards the English authorities that existed in the hearts of many GAA men.

Bloody Sunday was considered a turning point in the War of Independence, and moves were soon afoot to work towards a possible truce, despite the bad relations that obviously existed. On 11 July 1921 the Truce was agreed, and the negotiations that followed led to a new treaty being drawn up whereby Britain granted free-state status to twenty-six of the thirty-two counties, retaining six in the north of the country, and establishing the border that exists to this day.

THE BAN

The emergence of the new Irish Free State, promising as it did less turbulent days ahead, allowed the GAA to concentrate once again on its games. Everybody knew where the GAA stood, however – fully behind the republican ideals. Its hardline position was demonstrated by the ban it imposed on its members playing or even attending so-called 'foreign games', which essentially meant games that emanated from England.

The Ban is probably the single most controversial aspect of the GAA's colourful history. In place from the end of the nineteenth century, for decades it stood as testimony to the GAA's republican credentials and as a symbol of the independence the Association gained for Ireland's native games. In the eyes of critics it was evidence of a backward-thinking, insular body that had political motives and no understanding of the notion that sport is for all and that men and women should be free to play whatever games they wish.

The GAA had never been slow to implement bans. In 1885 a row with a rival athletics body led to a motion declaring that 'any athlete competing at meetings held under other laws than those of the Gaelic Athletic Association shall be ineligible to compete at meetings held under the GAA'. That ban was put in place but rescinded shortly afterwards. Interestingly, Archbishop Croke, the GAA's first patron, made his views on the ban mentality clear in a letter written in 1885, one year after the establishment of the GAA. He wrote:

> ...as a patron of the GAA, a lover of fair play all round and the enemy of every species of needless strife and estrangement among Irishmen, I would respectfully suggest to the Committee of management of the GAA the advisability of modifying their rules in the above particular, so as to allow all qualified athletes to compete for their prizes.

Man had walked on the moon by the time the GAA would fully go along with this sense of fair play.

While there were some unsuccessful attempts to have the Ban dropped in the 1920s, it wasn't until the 1950s that a significant number of GAA members really began to have second thoughts about it. It had always been attacked by outside critics, but the GAA grassroots were emphatically supportive of the stance in the early days. Indeed, in fairness to the GAA it should be said that the position they adopted on foreign games probably had as much to do with protecting their own games – which they had, after all, saved from extinction – as with an inherent dislike of other games or the long-established ill feeling towards the British.

Because of the hostile relationship that existed between England and Ireland for so much of the early part of the twentieth century – forged as it was by blood and tears – the existence of the Ban had never been a major issue for the GAA. But as more conciliatory attitudes developed and younger people, carrying less baggage from the past, though still largely loyal to the GAA's republican position, became more involved in the GAA, the Ban became a source of much discussion.

Many in the GAA found it difficult to defend the Ban against outside criticism, and from the 1950s onwards a debate about its justification was ongoing. The Ban had become an embarrassment. By the end of the 1960s its abolition looked likely. The average GAA man did not want to stand over such a policy. In any event, it had become quite farcical. For years players had defied it, playing soccer or rugby under false names, or even attending those and other sports in disguise.

At a GAA convention in 1971, the GAA's notorious Rule 27 – the Ban – was removed. A new charter was drawn up, reaffirming the Association's commitment to the goal of a united Ireland. This was an appeasement to anyone who was intent on mourning the death of the Ban.

In recent years the relationship between the GAA and so-called foreign games has improved substantially. Most leading GAA personnel would now be perfectly happy to be seen supporting soccer or rugby, and new generations find it hard to imagine a time when any other circumstances could have prevailed.

Although the heady days when it was deeply embroiled in politics, at a time of incredible political upheaval, are gone, the GAA still influences perceptions in the troubled political relationship between Britain and Ireland. Many decades after the Treaty and the partition of Ireland, the fighting continues over the six counties that constitute Northern Ireland. The GAA's police ban is still in place, with British soldiers and police officers (RUC) serving in Northern Ireland precluded by Rule 21 from playing Gaelic games. This ban is a source of much contention, and is seen by unionists and Protestants as evidence that the GAA is sectarian and has a clear political agenda, an agenda that would indeed be at one with that of the modern-day IRA. There is intense pressure on the GAA to rescind this ban, but to do so would require a majority vote at National Congress; there is no short-term sign of that happening yet.

Today the GAA concentrates on its games. Its claim that it has no political role is now much more credible than it ever was in the past. Yet as long as Rule 21 exists, and probably as long as there is conflict on Irish soil, the GAA will remain in the shadows of the political chambers. Stark and explosive evidence that sometimes sport and politics are indeed destined to intertwine.

11

THE INTERNATIONAL DIMENSION

It's a long way to go for a brawl. In the mid-1980s, however, the cream of Ireland's Gaelic footballers and the elite of Australian Rules football made regular trips across the world to beat each other up and quarrel over who had the best sport.

The Australians, who play a game not entirely dissimilar to Gaelic football, came to Ireland in 1984, and two years later, when the wounds had healed, the two countries battled it out in Australia. Two further showdowns took place in 1987 and 1990. The teams representing the two countries played a strange new game which incorporated some of the rules of Gaelic football, some of the rules of Australian Rules football, and, contrary to the brief given to the players, most of the rules of wrestling and boxing. Irish fans – elated at the prospect of Gaelic games gaining an international dimension, and beside themselves with joy that it involved frequent outbreaks of fighting – rose at unnatural hours of the morning to watch the Australian games live on television. The experiment lasted six years, and lives on now only on dusty video tapes and in the aching bones of the star players of a decade ago.

The experimental series between Australia and Ireland

had their critics, and some fans. For years GAA supporters have lamented the absence of international competition from Ireland's most played game. The lack of any significant international dimension in football (and hurling) denies players the chance to exhibit their talents on a world stage, and to compare themselves with contemporaries from other countries.

Gaelic football is eminently capable of thriving in its own little nook of course, but the dream, however far-fetched, of seeing the game spread to other countries has continued to live in the minds of some. These are people who perhaps wonder wistfully if soccer legend Pele might have been a great Gaelic footballer, or for that matter if a superstar in some other sport in a far-off country might have captivated us with his hurling skills. Questions without answers.

The Australia/Ireland Compromise Rules tests gave the GAA fraternity a chance to see Gaelic football, albeit in an altered form, played internationally. There was great excitement when the idea was first mooted. Star Gaelic footballers would finally get a reward of sorts, in the form of international recognition that previously seemed the preserve of their soccer counterparts.

The belief that some international arrangement involving Australia and Ireland and their games could be established had a precedent. Back in 1967 a team from Australia played two games in Ireland, against counties Meath and Mayo, with the visiting team winning both. The game combined the more popular and common aspects of the Australian game and Gaelic football. The following year Meath travelled to Australia and won all five of the matches on their tour. The Australians came back to Ireland later in 1968, winning two and drawing one of their three games. Kerry played five matches in Australia in 1970, winning all of them, including one in which an oval ball was used – proving that the sporting gods do smile on Kerrymen when distributing skills!

Meanwhile, as Gaelic football grew in popularity in Ireland, so too did Australian Rules football in Australia. The powers that be were attracted by the similarities that existed between the two games. Australian Rules football, an enormously popular and distinctive game in its country of origin, is without question the field game that most resembles Gaelic football.

Players can carry the ball in the hand, catching it (like 'fielding' in Gaelic) and transferring possession by the hand or through kicked passes. The game is an extremely physical contact sport, reminiscent of a Gaelic game. There are distinct differences between the two games, however. In Australian Rules football the players use an oval ball as in rugby, and there are no goalkeepers. There are four uprights at either end of the pitch, which is oval in shape. If the ball is passed through the centre uprights, a goal (worth six points) is awarded. A point is awarded when it is sent through either of the 'outer' sets of uprights. After a goal is scored, the ball is brought back to the centre of the field, where the game is restarted when the official bounces it off the ground. A small number of Gaelic footballers have travelled to Australia to take up the game, Dubliner Jim Stynes being by far the most successful. He has enjoyed a fantastic career in Australian football and is recognised as one of its greatest stars.

Duly attracted by the similarities, and their exploratory work done, the GAA and their Australian counterparts decided in the 1980s to organise international competition involving the two games. There were many reasons why it appeared to be a good idea. It would give players in both countries a chance to play international football. It would prove popular with fans, with national pride at stake. From the GAA's point of view, it would send positive signals to the large Irish community in Australia. Irish people have emigrated to Australia in vast numbers throughout the years and Gaelic football has long been played there by the emigrant Irish. By bringing GAA stars on tour to Australia, and by creating an international sport between their native and adopted countries, the GAA would be serving those emigrants well and generally developing the excellent sporting and cultural relations that existed between the two countries.

There didn't appear to be any strong case for not going ahead with the experiment. At worst, the games would have an exhibition-type value, rewarding the players and entertaining the fans. There were those who dismissed the idea as daft and condemned the attempt to wed two games that were not, in their eyes, suited to one another. The experiment went ahead, however. Common rules were drawn up and the whole exercise was labelled the Compromise Rules series.

As that title suggests, the plan involved compromise on both sides. The Irish would agree to play without goalkeepers. The shape of the ball would alternate – oval one day, round the next. The Australians had a rule whereby a player, on fielding the ball, could call a 'mark' – stopping the game on the spot to allow him to pick out a colleague with a free kick, as a 'reward' for the clean catch – and this was adopted by the Irish. Other minor changes were introduced, and suddenly the fusion of the two distinctive games had taken place. The child of an unlikely marriage had been born.

The first Compromise Rules series was played in Ireland in 1984. Australia beat Ireland by 70 points to 57 in the first test, but the Irish took the second by 80 points to 76. Australia won the series when they were victorious in the third international, winning by 76 to 71. Close games, interesting outcome. There was a sting in the tail, however, and a painful one at that. The games were notoriously violent on occasions. Certainly if any of the Irish teams had expected the Compromise Rules games to be 'friendlies', they were gravely mistaken.

Australian Rules football is the sort of physical contact sport that should have wrestlers as cheerleaders. The game is professional and is played, for the most part, by muscular, super-fit players who see gaining the upper hand on their opponent – physically – as an important early strategy. It is a game that the Gaelic football playing Irish of the nineteenth century would have approved of. Fist-fights are regular features. As the Australians are proud to boast, it is not a game for the weak. Brawls involving a dozen or so players are common in the native league.

The Australians, with their naturally competitive approach to sport, were predictably intent on gaining a physical edge on the Irish in those first tests. The Irish were completely taken by surprise, although they were not found wanting in later tests, adapting to the aggressive demands when re- quired. Indeed they could not have been successful if they had not 'squared up' to the Australians. The first series was notable for the outbreaks of fighting, at least some of which, in fairness, could be excused on the grounds that this was new territory for both sets of players. It was an explosive start to the experiment, and a fearsome quelling of any notion that the games would be easy-going exhibition affairs. It is fair to say that a majority of people in Gaelic football circles – well used to physical exchanges – were shocked by the ferocity of what they had seen.

The first series did produce some good football (as did subsequent ones) and the players, management and most of the fans enjoyed it overall; but the unmistakable image that was developing was of a brutally physical new game that left the GAA, like Frankenstein, wondering whether it had created a monster that was now out of control. Critics, including those who had predicted the worst, and those who gaily bounded on to the bandwagon, had a field day. Some commented that the cross-fertilisation of two independent games led to little more than a freak show, while subsequent critics included Mick O'Connell, the legendary Gaelic footballer considered by many to be the greatest ever, who went on record describing the whole experiment as a fiasco.

Of course nobody was going to miss the second series, which took place in Australia two years later and was televised live in Ireland. The home team won the first test in Perth but the Irish won the next two to take the series, matching Australia's achievement two years earlier of winning on foreign soil. Again, over-aggression was a feature of the games.

The 1987 series, played in Dublin, was won by the Australians, two tests to one, while the fourth and final series, played in Australia in 1990, was won by the Irish, again by two tests to one.

The experiment led to nothing permanent and the cycle of series has not resumed in the 1990s. By failing to revive it, the powers that be are indicating that it was a failed exercise. Both games thrive in their own countries; the game they gave birth to slumbers.

So what is its legacy? Looking back on it, it is clear that the countries were very well matched. An uncanny feature of the exchanges is that after twelve tests, both countries had six wins, and despite the fact that there was an occasional heavy defeat for either country, a mere fifteen points separates the teams when aggregate scores over the twelve games are taken into account (Ireland 680, Australia 665). Interestingly, both countries won two of the four series played, in each case triumphing on foreign soil. This suggests that, violence notwithstanding, the Compromise Rules experiment had something in its favour insofar as the representative teams were invariably evenly balanced.

Furthermore, for players to be selected on the Irish panel was a great honour, as it was for the Australians. For non-paid players, the perk of being brought to Australia for a few weeks was not to be dismissed either. If the experiment succeeded – and led to a regular fixture – there was the prospect of an international career, travel, further fame and new friendships.

The abiding image of the experiment, however, was one of violence, which too frequently overshadowed good play. Perhaps it was just not considered practical to continue a game that asked stars of another game to adapt to new rules, new styles. Ultimately, criticism of the experiment seems to have silenced its promoters. In any event, the GAA's version of Frankenstein's monster has not even coughed in recent years.

The Australia/Ireland Compromise Rules experiment has been the GAA's only attempt thus far to organise inter-national competition for Gaelic football, and the game essentially remains bereft of a worldwide flavour. The same may be said of hurling, although it too has had an irregular flirtation with a compromise game.

SHINTY/HURLING

The Scottish game of shinty is several hundred years old. It is a form of ground-hurling, like the Irish version *camánacht* which was played in Ireland in the past but died out when it gave way to the style of hurling we know today. Of course ground-hurling is still a feature of hurling but in shinty it is the only style allowed. The stick used in shinty is different from a hurley in that it is not designed to balance the ball (as happens during a solo run) and in fact it resembles a hockey stick. However, shinty possesses enough similarities to Irish hurling to justify occasional compromise internationals between Scotland and Ireland.

The compromise game is not very imaginatively called 'hurling-shinty' and the first international was played in the 1920s at the famous Tailteann Games, a popular sporting festival at the time. While an international game took place in 1933, there was no further resumption until 1972. An annual international has taken place every year since 1993, with the venue alternating between Scotland and Ireland.

The most recent marriage of the games' rules has resulted in matches being played on a pitch 100 yards wide and 160 yards long, with fourteen-a-side teams and a goal and uprights (for points) as in hurling. Hurling has had to make concessions, however, to a game that has no aerial action. No player other than the goalkeeper can handle the ball, robbing the game of the spectacular catches that are a feature of hurling. This 'no handling' rule greatly restricts the Irish players' ability to guide points between the uprights. A shot that is struck off the ground and goes over the crossbar is worth a point; if it is struck directly off the ground from a free, two points are awarded. While the internationals are no doubt enjoyable and novel experiences for the players, they have made no impression on fans, and there is little public appetite for the games.

Apart from when it compromises and becomes a bedfellow of shinty, hurling, like Gaelic football, has no other international aspect, probably because the rest of the world thinks the Irish are mad even to attempt such a game. In any other country the idea of thirty men battling for a tiny ball with large sticks – which they can swing in the air and on the ground – would be dismissed as the rantings of a fool.

The irony is that people from other countries who have attended Gaelic games or been introduced to them on television have marvelled at the skill levels, the intensity of the battles, and the entertainment value that is provided, especially in hurling. In recent years, for example, Manchester United manager Alex Ferguson and some of his players attended a major game in Croke Park, while on one occasion in the 1990s a group of professional American footballers witnessed hurling in the flesh. Alex Ferguson and his highly-paid English Premiership football stars were flabbergasted by the pace, skill and physical intensity of Gaelic football; the Americans were rendered almost speechless when asked on radio for their views on what they had seen.

Now that the world has seen just how exciting and relatively safe hurling is – and how skilful its protagonists are – it is too late. It is unlikely that any other nation could catch up with the Irish, who in fairness have had over 2,000 years of a start.

It looks, therefore, as if Ireland's unique games are destined never to develop internationally. But the world is discovering the games more and more, with television broadcasting hurling and football to countless countries across the globe. Perhaps in time other countries will be simply unable to resist the temptation to make their own hurleys and to play catch and kick with the footballs they currently reserve for soccer.

Meanwhile, there is an interesting postscript to the Australian experiment. On 8 January 1998 the *Irish Independent* speculated that the international dimension Gaelic games enjoyed in its battles with the Australians might yet be revisited. The paper reported that a one-off game between Melbourne Football Club and an Irish selection, to honour Jim Stynes, was being touted. The report added that this could give the international series a kick-start. A dramatic return of the Frankenstein game would be a blow to the critics who saw it off – and would probably mean many more blows for the men sent into battle!

12

TO PAY OR NOT TO PAY?

Should GAA players be paid? Ask the thirty-two-year-old shopkeeper who is lying face down on a frozen patch of earth where grass used to live. His face, woven into the bitter ground at this moment, sports a three-inch gash from which droplets of blood are peering. His legs are aching with soreness, delivered by a crashing tackle in the first two minutes of this training session, and his chest, pressed against the partly-frozen turf, feels as if it has been attacked by a giant cheese-grater. He feels his groin to seek re-assurance that everything special to him is still in place. His fingers feel like icicles.

He slowly turns his head until he can see the spot beside the goal where he was lying in muck and filthy rainwater last week. Amazing how the weather changes. From miserable to brutal. All he can hear is, 'Gerry ... don't take all night to get up ... for Christ's sake!' He rises slowly. Michelle is getting £20 for the night to keep the shop open. She's a nice quiet girl. The kids will be in bed when he gets back. Anne will be engrossed in a film and it will be too late to explain what's happening in it, even during the ad break. He'll probably pay Michelle, throw the gear in the back kitchen, have a quick cup of tea, look in on the kids, feel his face and go to bed. The shop has to be open at 7 a.m.

The vexed question of whether or not GAA players should be paid has been around for a while, and is unlikely to go away. The GAA remains an amateur association, well over a hundred years after its foundation, but is finding it increasingly difficult to justify that stance in the modern fast-moving world.

Most traditionalists would be appalled at any notion of going professional – apart from reneging on its past, the notion of paying players would be uncomfortably close to copying soccer – yet the case for professionalism arises as a direct result of the phenomenal success of the Association. The players have been taking a semi-professional approach to training for years, arguably in response to the demands of fans; the general standard of play has thus improved; the games therefore attract larger crowds, and television companies become more interested. Financial support from government has also been forthcoming.

Thus, the GAA's finances have been boosted dramatically, and because of the players' increased efforts and sacrifices, and the perception that their masters are rolling in cash, the demand grows for players to be paid.

To be fair to the GAA, the Association has consistently used its income well. The same cannot be said of the FAI, the governing body of soccer in Ireland, which still has no national stadium despite the millions of pounds gained from the successes of the Irish soccer team in the World Cups of 1990 and 1994. By contrast, the GAA has acted wisely in putting back into its grassroots the money it has taken in. In so doing, it continues to make its outstanding contribution to the fabric of Irish life: providing games and facilities for the youth, developing the talents of its players, contributing to the social and cultural development of the country. The

Association has consistently improved its premier stadium, Croke Park (at the expense in recent times of attending to its clubs, some allege), and a controversial £20 million which the GAA received from government in 1997 will go towards the continued development of the stadium into one of the world's finest sporting venues. The question of rewarding players may have been ignored but no one can accuse the GAA of failing to reinvest the fruits of its success.

Club players benefit from the spreading of those funds when their local facilities and grounds are enhanced, but inter-county stars – the high-profile players who bring crowds to Croke Park and send them home spellbound – do not. They are not paid for the simple reason that, whatever its commercial success, the Association remains loyal to its amateur status. It is a noble and defensible stance but for many years now it has been widely questioned by people who believe that for a variety of reasons inter-county players deserve to be paid.

The most obvious reason is the enormous sacrifices the players make. The pressure on players in the 1990s is intense – and starkly at variance with what was the norm in previous eras. When the GAA was formed in 1884 its primary function was after all to revive Irish pastimes. Football and hurling were played largely for fun, and the only sacrifices made by players were the long walks or cycles to the venues – journeys they were in fact happy to undertake. Times were innocent and the GAA bank account was humble.

While the decades that followed saw interest in the games grow and attendances at big matches increase dramatically, it was not until the 1970s that players really began to make the superhuman efforts off the field that now represent the strongest case for their being financially rewarded. There had been collective training in the 1940s – when All-Ireland final teams spent a week or so together in preparation for the big game – but by and large it was not until the 1970s that full-scale training, not unlike that of soccer professionals, became part of the GAA set-up.

In the 1970s training became virtually an all-year commitment, with the old days of 'a few laps around the field' a couple of nights a week banished to the past. New, sophisticated routines were developed, with an emphasis on skill and tactics and a focused approach to stamina and fitness-building. Such training levels became the norm and the nature of Gaelic football had been changed forever.

Indeed the 1980s and 1990s have been notable for the emphasis on training and preparation for games, and it is not unusual in the current age for players to be running up mountains at 6 a.m.!

To win an All-Ireland title in the present era, a county team has to be extraordinarily fit, fast and strong. To reach those levels, family life, work commitments and social lives all suffer. When the players who make this phenomenal effort see the GAA taking in record gate receipts as a direct result, it is easy to see why many of them resent the fact that no financial return is forthcoming.

In effect, what players receive in return for their efforts in the current era amounts to travelling expenses in instances where they have to drive long distances to training sessions, a meal after the match, and a lot of backslapping. This is a mere covering of their costs. Of course, some star players do get invitations to present medals, make speeches, open shops and bars. There might be a few pounds exchanged. Managers too are increasingly being 'looked after' with good expenses. No wages, of course, just a few bob for your trouble. A step in the right direction, some would say.

Of course they get enjoyment too, but is it enough? What

other sporting body in the world would expect its stars to train so vigorously, often in appalling weather, reaching fitness levels on a par with professionals in other sports, then to compete with unparalleled passion in an All-Ireland campaign which, by its knock-out nature, may only last for a single game? Players who risk injury, change work schedules, sacrifice time with their families; who are invariably exposed to scorn, abuse and ridicule from fans and in some cases from the media if they are adjudged not to have performed well. In this day and age, such players do not feel it is unreasonable to expect to be afforded more respect.

Those who play Gaelic games at a high level, keeping turnstiles from going rusty in the process, see stars from other sports earning huge sums of money. Kevin Moran was a famous Gaelic football player with Dublin; in the 1970s he left Ireland to pursue a career in soccer with Manchester United. He was a great Gaelic footballer and a great soccer player. Essentially, he was a great athlete. If he were playing today, he would earn perhaps £20,000 a week with Manchester United; if he had stayed with Dublin he would have to perfect the art of combining work and play.

It is not just the knowledge that their peers in other sports are attracting large wages that galls many GAA stars; they are also understandably envious of the sponsorship revolution. Stars of soccer, rugby, golf and other sports can now earn spectacular amounts of money by endorsing various products or services.

That many of the top GAA players in Ireland have an envious eye on these stars, who all seem to dress in designer suits and drive Porsches, and that they resent the lack of distribution by the GAA of its increased profits, seems clear. It should be said that the vast majority of players aren't obsessed with the idea of going professional – indeed many would oppose it. What they do want is greater recognition of the enormous effort they put in. They do not want to be taken for granted.

GAA players have frequently hinted and sometimes stated publicly that they are not seeking wages of the kind soccer players are accustomed to. Other ways of rewarding them could be explored.

One which the GAA is set to introduce is a players' pool. In this scenario players will charge the media for interviews: all monies collected will be pooled, and distributed amongst players. While star players will naturally be in greater demand by the media than lower-profile players, the even distribution of the total amount in the pool will ensure that media-shy or less sought-after players will not lose out. Of course, the proceeds will be modest enough.

Another welcome development (in 1997) was the decision to remove any ban on players endorsing products and being paid for advertising. This had already crept into the game and the players and fans, on the whole, had no difficulty with it; stuffy officials throughout the country who detested any move away from outright amateurism did, however. An enlightened decision has now been made. While allowing players to endorse products for financial gain will benefit a handful of stars, the obvious drawback is that in a small country only a few will be in demand and the vast majority of players will not benefit. Ultimately, the dilemma may only be resolved by paying players a small wage.

Neither permitting players to endorse products nor the setting up of players' media pools will cost the GAA financially; paying players would. There are some who will argue that, its improved financial status notwithstanding, the Association could not afford to pay players. But you can usually achieve something if your heart is in it. The GAA top brass – those administrators based at GAA headquarters in Croke Park – have long been paid for their work for the Association.

It is therefore not difficult to spot contradictions in all of this. If administrators are paid, shouldn't players be? If the Association is taking in huge sums of money, shouldn't a part of this financial windfall be shared with the players, the very people who are attracting the fans in the first place? Players could be paid something; certainly more than nothing. The suggestion that the Association cannot afford it does not hold up. Those making this argument point out that there are only a certain number of big games in Croke Park every year, and that the hype about the income from those games overlooks the fact that the Association has large expenses all year round. They also pose questions. Who would be paid? Just inter-county players? If so, how many in each county? Would there be a wage ceiling? Would a transfer system, as in soccer, inevitably follow, with players having agents, money becoming their master, and the traditional reason you played Gaelic – for pride in your parish – suffering? Would smaller counties be able to compete with larger, wealthier ones?

Many in the GAA oppose professionalism on historic grounds. They won't pay because they don't want to. Michael Cusack's shadow is in the background. Their fathers weren't paid. Play the game for pride, for the love of it, because you want to. We are amateurs. Play for the parish or don't bother at all.

Others would say that the GAA is in fact amateur in name only. The players are amateurs in that they are not being paid, but in every other respect the GAA has the veneer of professionalism about it. It may be argued that the Association has purposely avoided change on this crucial issue despite the fact that it has changed in other ways on and off the field.

It should be said that while the GAA does not reward its players in a significant, tangible way, many benefits do accrue for star players. Apart from the celebrity status they enjoy during their career, many find that their fame serves them well at the end of their playing days.

Numerous players have opened pubs or other businesses, cashing in on their status as household names. Others have embarked on political careers which at the very least have been boosted by their sporting endeavours. Indeed, the political parties are constantly trying to pressurise recently retired footballers into contesting elections. The public often responds to a GAA star's name on the ballot paper as though the player were the answer to the country's political woes, miraculously unearthed after having squandered years pursuing a football across the pitches of Ireland. Quite simply, being a star footballer or hurler can be a great asset in career terms. The GAA may not open bank accounts for you, but it can open doors. Several ex-players have become members of the Dáil (the Irish Parliament). Ex-Taoiseach Jack Lynch was a Cork hurling legend, and former Cavan football great John Wilson became Tánaiste (Deputy Prime Minister).

As to the future, it seems likely that players will have more and more money in their pockets, through endorsements, players' pools, maybe even wages. The GAA will probably manage this while still claiming to be amateur.

Meanwhile, a shopkeeper with a sore face and £20 less in the till opens a small shop on a bitterly cold morning. Manchester United star Roy Keane's facial cut would be attended to by a team of doctors. His training session would be over in the afternoon, not held on a dark frosty night. He doesn't have a shop on which his livelihood depends and doesn't need a nice quiet Michelle to run it for the few hours he's away. If he did and he had to pay her, he'd have plenty left over from that week's wages. Then he'd get into his Porsche.

13
——

THE PEOPLE WHO MAKE THE GAA

Some of them drive BMWs, some drive the team bus and get no thanks for it, and many more just drive their friends mad. The GAA thrives because a combination of different people are so deeply devoted to ensuring that the national movement keeps moving.

Most of the people who make the GAA the success that it is are acting in a voluntary capacity, although the Association's Croke Park based administrators are paid, which is fair enough as they are working as full-time employees.

GAA affairs in each county are governed by a County Board, made up of delegates from the various clubs, who have been elected to these posts by members of the clubs. The delegates in turn elect a County Board executive, whose members run all aspects of the GAA in that county, while remaining answerable to the rank-and-file members of the County Board.

The typical County Board member, like the typical club member, is a hard-working Gael who devotes endless hours to voluntary work for the benefit of the games in his or her area. Some members of a County Board executive will in time rise to positions of power on the provincial councils. Each provincial council elects delegates to the Ardchomhairle (national governing body or Central Council), whose decisions are made at Annual Congress. The GAA elects a national president every four years.

Throughout the years the GAA has been fortunate to have attracted some outstanding administrators and visionary presidents. Dick Blake became general secretary of the GAA before the end of the nineteenth century and is credited with inspiring many positive developments within the Association.

Outstanding general secretaries of the twentieth century include long-serving administrators Luke O'Toole, Padraig O'Caoimh and Sean O'Siochain. Tipperary man Maurice Davin was the GAA's first president and had the unique distinction of holding office for two separate terms.

Most GAA clubs have a number of unsung heroes or heroines. For every player who places majestic points between the posts – to the acclaim of the fans – there is a largely anonymous middle-aged man who is happily married and forever loyal to his one partner – the GAA. He lives in a small house beside the local pitch and considers 'the Park' his pride and joy. He lines the pitch, attends to and locks the clubhouse and always knows the result of the obscure Under-14 match the previous evening, in which his club was not even involved.

Managers and team selectors, more often than not ex-players who cannot divorce themselves from the game, make enormous sacrifices and are often rewarded only with stinging criticism and the label of having failed. More anonymous in the GAA are the countless men and women who devote a large part of their lives to coaching young children in the basic skills of the game, usually without acclaim or recognition. Of course, in their eyes the sheer enjoyment gained by them and the children might be success enough. Like the parents who drive children to training and matches, or the man who tends to the grounds, they are unsung heroes: people who will never touch the Sam Maguire Cup unless an All-Ireland winning player brings it to their club's annual dinner dance. These are people who hardly have time to dream what it must be like to hold the trophy aloft as the captain of a winning team. They never make headlines, but on lonely fields across the country their joyous, fulfilling love affair blossoms as they patiently guide the stars of the future.

THE PLAYERS

The other group of people who help make the GAA are of course the players. To be a county player is to have gained an exalted position in Irish society. Indeed, to be a star at club level is to guarantee yourself admiring and envious glances in the parish – and that's just from the men to start with. Top football players achieve great fame in Ireland, even if fame alone does not pay the bills. Star players are feted in their native towns and villages; masterminding success for club or county transforms ordinary men into kings.

Celebrity status – at various levels – is enjoyed by most of the players. Some may find it tiresome. Unlike in other sports, GAA stars mix easily with the fans, as befits the game's amateur status.

THE MEN IN BLACK

Referees also help keep the GAA in business, although a lot of fans and quite a few players will not always agree with that notion. The men in black are assisted by linesmen who, incredible as it might seem, are often drawn from the two clubs in action, leaving them open to angry accusations of bias from the 'can only see their own team' brigade.

The 'can only see their own team' brigade can be fans or

managers, selectors or substitutes, but the one thing they cannot be is impartial. They are an intrinsic part of the GAA. Every officiating decision is received with horror, every misdemeanour by a member of the opposing team grossly exaggerated. The logic is simple. The referee is obviously related to three of the other team's players, is dating the captain's sister, shares a business with their manager and was born half a mile from their parish boundary. This logic is accepted by most in their midst, all of whom resume life as perfectly normal people within a few hours of the final whistle.

MEDIA STARS

The media have their own personalities of course, people whose reputations have been built upon their coverage of GAA affairs. The two most famous GAA commentators of all time are the late Mícheál O'Hehir and the present-day legend in his own lifetime, Mícheál Ó Muircheartaigh. O'Hehir's fame and status owed much to his undoubted brilliance as a commentator but the fact that his rise preceded the arrival of television and coincided with the great days of radio was a huge factor in creating his legend.

The picture has often been painted for younger generations. In the Ireland of the 1940s and 1950s there was no television, and not every house had a radio (then called 'wireless'). Households that did have one had to make it their business to have food and drink too, for each Sunday during the summer neighbours would congregate in houses fortunate enough to have the magic messengers. The wonderfully distinctive voice they heard bringing the drama of big football games to the kitchens of rural Ireland was that of Mícheál O'Hehir.

For years he was the eyes of the public, who felt they could see the action unfold, so inspired were his commentaries. His most famous broadcast was in 1947 when Kerry and Cavan met in the Polo Grounds in New York. The match over-ran, and national broadcasters RTÉ looked set to close the link until O'Hehir pleaded on air, 'Give me five minutes more.' He didn't know if anyone could hear him, but he continued with the commentary. The lines had been left open. O'Hehir got his five extra minutes and more deserved space in Irish folklore.

O'Hehir was as effective when he switched to television, and it was heartbreaking for himself, his family and his fans when, within days of his being due to commentate on his one hundredth All-Ireland final (hurling and football) fate intervened in the form of illness. He never returned to the microphone but a glittering fifty-year career and a momentous ninety-nine final commentaries had earned him a place – without his ever having to kick a ball – in any GAA Hall of Fame.

Mícheál Ó Muircheartaigh commentates on radio only but does it so superbly that a television would seem almost superfluous. This poet of the airwaves allows you to feel the passion of the game while also telling you who the corner-forward's mother voted for in the 1960s or where the goalkeeper met his fiancée.

The print media have played an extremely important role in bringing to the public news of GAA games and affairs, especially in the early days of the Association's existence. In recent times some players have taken up the pen, but most of the great GAA writers never won fame on the playing fields. Instead, from behind their keyboards, they've played their own very important part in making the GAA a success.

The Fans

Vying with the players as key people who keep the GAA going are the fans. The GAA fan shows what the games mean to him or her in different ways, but as an example of sheer passionate anticipation I think with fondness of the man I saw walking to Croke Park a couple of years ago, and whose ever-widening step I wrote of at the time:

He's about fifty, small in build, and stocky. He was probably a handful for many's a corner-back in his day. Everything is conveyed by his walk. He doesn't know whether to break into an undignified trot or just maintain his urgent, excited walking pace. The result is that he is doing neither properly, but instead skipping along, his feet occasionally making contact with the pavement below. He is wearing jeans and runners and the mandatory Dublin jersey ... and strapped around his waist is a blue Dublin scarf ... it's his sense of anticipation that captivates. We all feel it, but he is like a child who has been told that his father has relented and he can after all host a birthday party. As he skips along, willing Croke Park to move towards him, there's an air about his person that dismisses all possible thoughts of mortgage repayments, marital rows, time's relentless passage or any other impending woes. Dublin versus Meath in Croker, the sun shining, the minutes ticking away. Minutes later I am delayed by another set of traffic lights ... he is passing me, the step even more of a hop, the single-minded march unchecked towards Croker, his

valley of dreams. I do believe that at this moment
he may indeed be the world's happiest man.

ARMCHAIR CRITICS

Others who help make the GAA a success are the armchair
critics who condemn the Association at every opportunity.
They dismiss the GAA as a 'Grab-All Association', which they
allege makes a huge amount of money but does little in
return. The accusation does not stand up. The armchair
critics are entitled to their point of view and are doubtless
correct on occasion, but some of them are so extreme and
cynical that in effect they act as an incentive to hard-working,
decent GAA people.

THE MAN WHO MAKES THE GAA

I often think, however, that the man who really makes the
GAA is the character in a short story by the great Kerry writer
John B. Keane. Our hero goes to the pub after Mass, and it
must be said that there is nothing unusual in that. He has a
number of pints of Guinness before going home for a very
large dinner. He then decides, after a short sleep, that he will
cycle to a low-key game some miles away. This being the
GAA, however, he ends up playing in goal as one team is
short of players and our hero proves a willing volunteer or
innocent victim. Luckily his team does all the attacking, and
the only save he has to make involves his falling upon a weak
shot.

The story is beautifully told, and paints a picture of the
game in rural Ireland that most Gaels would recognise. John
B. Keane concludes that our hero is the world's greatest
goalkeeper, which, in a sense, he is. He is certainly one of
the people who, as much as any great player or visionary
administrator, makes the GAA. He may be prone to falling

asleep after a few pints and he may not run the GAA or star on its greatest stage, but 'the world's greatest goalkeeper' certainly does make the GAA the peculiar, complex, but wonderful phenomenon that it is.

14

THE GAA: A WAY OF LIFE

If you were asked to prepare a thesis on the Irish, one of the best things you could do (apart from saying no) would be to observe every aspect of a major Gaelic football or hurling occasion. The GAA and its games have an ability to lure people from their houses, not to return until several hours have passed and countless stories have been penned.

It happens on Sundays, at local parish level, on county final day, on the occasion of provincial showdowns and, most vividly of all, on All-Ireland final day. To observe the relationship between the people and their games is to gain an insight into the GAA's profound cultural impact on the Irish.

The day starts many days previously. In the mind. Those who are passionate about the local team have been dreaming for days about their chances in the big game. The team has been selected in the mind, beautiful goals have been scored, points have been recorded from amazing angles, and inspired substitutions have been made at precisely the correct time.

The game is anticipated with excitement and fear. Looked forward to and dreaded. Victory is briefly fantasised about; defeat is given considerable thought. Nerves are such that the butterflies in the stomach are organising reunions.

In the old days, on the night before the game, the man

of the house would go to the local pub by bicycle or on foot. There he would ponder on the big game's outcome in the company of the men he once played with. 'What time are ye going at?' and 'How will they do?' – the mundane openers – would soon be replaced by an intense analysis of all that mattered in the life of the parish. Each new mouthful of stout would tear shreds off the present and tomorrow, and the past would be revisited, when full-backs were built like mountains and balls were majestically dragged from the clouds.

These days it is the same – if different! The pubs and the mode of transport may have changed, but the sons and daughters carry on the tradition, feel the passion, have inherited the pain and the joy. Now the fathers and grand-fathers have vacated their high stools. They live on in black and white photographs of the 1930s team, behind the bar counter: young, strong men, their arms folded, standing beside the grinning man in suit and cap whose name the caption-writer did not know.

Today the pubs are sophisticated, buzzing, and alive with the youth of the parish. Ireland is a different country, more liberal, more cosmopolitan, more welcoming to outside cultures and influences. But Gaelic games remain as emotional directors of a large percentage of the people.

Before the big games of today – parish derby, county final or All-Ireland – the nervous, hopeful, tormented pre-match debates rage as in the past. The Irish, young and old, love to talk, and nowhere more so than in the traditional social centre, the public house. When the talk is of an upcoming football or hurling match, it is animated, spirited, hopeful and often unrealistic. The men who will tog out tomorrow are all expected to play great games by the men who drink tonight! That's just the way it is. They are representing us, and we are expectant.

On the actual morning of the match the observer will notice that the game is influencing everything. Farmers tend to their chores early; there's a bigger crowd than usual at first Mass. Players leave their children to the underage game, the starting time of which has been brought forward because of the big game.

If it's a county match, the previews in the papers are scanned over a large breakfast. Reassurance or doubts will follow, the words of a journalist, who may know very little about the protagonists, taking on a credence they rarely merit. It's good to see your own county's name in big print. It's your day. The heart beats faster. It's time to get the show on the road.

All the way to the match venue, the spirits are boosted by the colourful presence of flags and banners outside virtually every household. It's a sight unique to the GAA. The parish or county team is representing that area solely, whereas in soccer a club can have fans from anywhere.

The atmosphere at GAA grounds on big match day is one of the most endearing aspects of Gaelic games. There are no police on horseback, as is the norm outside English soccer grounds, where for some years (though not of late) hooliganism has afflicted the game.

Instead, fans of opposing sides mingle to a degree that makes the whole GAA experience special. It is remarkable testimony to the fundamental decency of a race and to the ability of Gaelic games to bring people together rather than drive a wedge between them, as is the unhappy experience of some other sports. On the approach roads to the grounds, thousands of fans of the participating teams walk side by side, singing, chanting, indulging in good-natured banter. A fight between rival sets of supporters is unheard of. Harmony and hope reign.

There are other performers on the stage, all of whom play a part in making the big match day special. 'Hats, scarves or rosettes' is the never-ending refrain of the world-weary men and women who pitch their stalls along the route, supplying fans with their team's 'colours' and their own pockets with the coins that will sustain their livelihood. The result doesn't matter to them, although a draw, requiring a replay, wouldn't be bad, would it?

Also kept busy are the publicans, for whom big match day is a massive bonanza. Thousands of well-behaved customers descend on them, thirsty for drink and conversation – and that's just before the game! At provincial finals it is a common sight to see pubs throughout the host town literally overflowing with customers.

I remember attending my first Munster football final just a few years ago, and the rich, colourful human tapestry was a sight to behold. In my book *The Search for Sam* I wrote about the scene in that great tourist location, Killarney, reflecting on 'bemused foreigners in cars trying to weave past hundreds of Cork fans, drinks in hand, arms linked across the street'. With the sun shining, the throw-in looming, old friendships renewed and frenetic conversation amongst strangers – now friends – about the upcoming game, it is a feeling that the Irish live for. From that particular year in Munster I recall a scene in the Killarney Towers Hotel that summed up the amazing coming together of opposing fans that makes the Gaelic experience unique.

In *The Search for Sam* I described it thus:

> ... it's two o'clock, and the pre-match craic is great. There's a Mark Chapman (John Lennon's assassin) lookalike in the company of a group of mad Corkmen. And he's an American and all! He

is getting a unique taste of Munster final day. An uncomplimentary verse is being sung about some of the Cork players, in which they are described as something that rhymes with 'tankers'. Then a more tasteful, impromptu singsong starts. A group of Kerrymen are singing 'The Rose of Tralee'. It is necessary to stand on stools for maximum effect. As they sing, they wave their fists in the air and stare across at the grinning Cork contingent. When they finish, they're about to restart but are thwarted as the Cork group break into 'The Banks of My Own Lovely Lee' (the Cork anthem). When this rendition has ended, the Kerrymen break into applause. Both groups end up embracing and singing 'The Fields of Athenry'. The American who looks like Mark Chapman is at the counter, and I'd swear his head is shaking. 'Can't wait till I tell the folks back home about this!'

Another regular feature of the excursion to big matches down through the years has been the 'picnic in the boot' experience (generally more popular than the 'referee in the boot' experience referred to earlier, when an unpopular official was dispatched to a car boot to allow him to reflect on his alleged sins). The picnic isn't actually held in the boot of the car, but the food is. Somewhere along the route the contents are taken out and propped on the car bonnet, and mother, father, children and grandparents proceed to dine, while waving deliriously as neighbours who haven't acknowledged them in months honk their horns as they pass.

This particular tradition is dying out to a degree but for many years it encapsulated the social event that a big GAA game was and is. The whole family travelled, as did the dinner. The county were in action; there was nowhere else on God's earth that self-respecting people should be, other than at their side.

Finally, the game is under way. The pride of the parish or county are on the field. You are supporting them, but you have an absolute right to condemn them in forceful terms. After the mandatory greetings of familiar faces in the crowd, all eyes focus on the action. The passion of the fans is what keeps the games alive and in such fine health. So many different emotions are unleashed. There is so much at stake. It is almost unbearable to watch. The roar of the crowd is deafening, the tension incredible, the fear of failure wrestling frantically with the tantalising prospect of possible victory.

Whichever way the result goes, for most fans the post-mortems are invariably held inside and outside overflowing public houses, where virtually every kick of the game is reflected upon. Men who have seen it all before – and whose side has lost – shake their heads knowingly, as though no words are necessary, their eyes meeting. 'What could you say about that performance?' one of them will ask dismissively, desperate to be the first to castigate the local team. Having indicated to all and sundry that there's nothing that can be said about the display, he proceeds to use every word in the English language and many that are outside it to condemn the efforts of the county's braves, while his unfortunate victim contemplates moving to another part of the bar.

During these marathon post-mortems on the game, the GAA's own unique language is employed, just as it will have been at the match itself. Gaelic games and the drama that surrounds them have been responsible for many new words, phrases and sayings which offer respite from the variety of expletives that usually abound during 'GAA conversations'.

'Over the bar' refers to the essential practice of scoring a point (over the crossbar), but can also be applied to the state some of the GAA diehards find themselves in by pub closing time. The GAA was synonymous with non-drinkers (pioneers) in the early days but new generations are winning the desperate battle to make up ground in this regard. A GAA diehard? This is not a Bruce Willis fan (not necessarily at least) but a person who is so passionate about football and/or hurling that it virtually dominates his life.

Thus when a government finance minister grants the GAA £20million for the development of Croke Park – while other sports and other causes watch in despair – you should avoid raising the apparent unfairness of this with the GAA diehard. You might as well tell a politician not to go to a funeral. The diehard (in most cases) will defend the Association to the end, often ignoring its weaknesses and shortcomings. He's a 'GAA man through and through' or a 'GAA man out and out'. He watches soccer occasionally (his father didn't, mind you) but 'can't understand anyone enjoying a game where there's hardly any scores and that is played, for the most part, by wimps'.

Most GAA men enjoy seeing a good fight at a game. This desire is frequently satisfied. When asked by someone who missed the game if it was any good, they will say, 'No, but there was mighty skelpin' at it.' 'Skelpin'', broadly speaking, means punching other players, preferably those on the opposing team.

The 'hurler on the ditch' is not a player who has been unceremoniously landed in the middle of the ditch by a fearsome shoulder-charge, but a person who criticises from a distance without getting involved. A 'useless shower' is not a reference to inadequate post-match facilities for players, although they're not uncommon. 'Useless shower' is the carefully thought-out label bestowed by fans on a team perceived to have let them down.

This is the GAA. The games that some people virtually live for. No words are necessary if you visit their houses. The hurley or ball and seasoned boots will be lying in the back kitchen. If they are not there, 'He's below in the field.' 'I don't know where they're playing today,' his wife might say with mock weariness, 'it seems like they have a game every day. If it's not a game, it's training.' The hurler or footballer, or the fan, have become bonded to the hurley, the football or the game. The games become a part of you. They take possession of your being, your family, your house, your life. Then life continues, with the GAA man and his game welded together, consciously and subconsciously.

One conclusion of our imaginary thesis would surely be that Gaelic games provide a great outlet for the people, in sporting and social terms. For those affected by the games, smitten by them, they play a huge part in their lives. 'The GAA spread like a prairie fire,' said a proud Michael Cusack of the Association's early years. In Irish hearts, the fire still burns brightly.

15

LOOKING TO THE FUTURE

As the GAA reaches a new millennium, it can reflect with justifiable pride on its great achievements. The Association has countless critics and genuine shortcomings but these cannot detract from its phenomenal success.

Looking back over its entire history the outstanding achievement of the GAA is that it has helped shape the very development of a people and a country. Without the GAA, would millions of Irish people have enjoyed the sporting, social and cultural expression offered by Gaelic games? Of course not. The Association has become a national movement, a driving force behind the people, a giant parental figure to the youth of the country.

It has succeeded beyond the wildest dreams of its founders in reviving the native Irish games. The madness that prevailed, quaint though it was, when our ancestors crossed fields and swamps in pursuit of a ball – and a game to call their own – has been replaced, in Gaelic football, by a beautiful sport that celebrates uniquely Irish attributes.

What can we say about hurling? It is not to detract from Gaelic football to repeat that the clash of the ash makes a powerful claim to be the world's most skilful, most exciting, most exhilarating game. Centuries ago it was famously labelled by a visiting writer as 'cricket for savages', which might have been accurate were it not for the fact that it bears no resemblance to cricket and has never been played by savages. But perhaps you couldn't blame him. Today, it is more like a sport from God, and however uninhibited the approach may have been in former days, the game evolved from there and thus owes its glorious existence to the men who, all those years ago, wielded the ash with passion and sheer love for what they were doing.

The GAA revived hurling and football, developed them, and then had to react swiftly to a phenomenal growth in membership and, later, to the challenges presented by a changing Ireland. Football and hurling currently thrive; camogie and handball are growing in popularity. The Scor talent competitions remain appealing to sections of the Association's membership, despite the counter-attractions that have emerged over the years.

The GAA's success should be judged by the health and standard of its games and by the size and mood of its membership. It scores well on all counts. The organisation's achievement may also be seen in the superb facilities that exist all over Ireland as a direct result of its work. Primarily sporting facilities, they also act as venues for social and cultural events. The Association has spent wisely and acted with a sense of sporting and social responsibility.

Of course the GAA has also enjoyed great commercial success. The popularity of its games has led to ever greater attendances, increases in revenue and the consequent urge to develop further its premier stadium, Croke Park. This will become one of the world's top stadia over the coming years with the completion of its multi-million-pound face-lift and expansion.

The GAA has been accused of sheer greed in relation to

its policy on Croke Park. In the 1990s the Association controversially reserved large sections of a new stand to accommodate corporate boxes. Some see this development as symbolic of the Association's apathy towards rank-and-file diehards who scramble desperately for elusive tickets while the GAA top brass entertain their corporate 'friends'.

Although Gaelic games are far from immune to unsportsmanlike behaviour, the Association has generally played a positive role in helping to develop the character of the people who play its games. The GAA instills positive values in the youth, such as pride in their parish, discipline and an appreciation of fair play and things Irish.

The Association's greatest service to the people is the joy that it has brought. The playing fields, from the humblest on a soft winter's day to a packed Croke Park on a hot summer's evening, hum with the sweet sound of amateur athletes treading the turf in homage to the football and the *sliotar*. There have been millions of people over the years who have never worn football boots or held a hurley, but whose lives have been made infinitely happier by the excitement, drama and anticipation that Gaelic games annually bring.

The GAA therefore has every reason to be both proud and happy as it embraces the new millennium. However, it has no reason to be smug, complacent or lazy. Extraordinary challenges lie ahead. For all its success the Gaelic Athletic Association faces countless headaches in the years ahead – and an uncertain future.

To squander its enviable position as Ireland's leading sporting body would perhaps seem impossible. After all, it has excellent foundations in place. Yet poor judgement or taking the eye off the ball, so to speak, could threaten the continued prosperity of the GAA in the twenty-first century. At best the Association will have to make painful and possibly unpopular decisions, perhaps reneging on its past and certainly moving adroitly to respond to the challenges of a rapidly changing world.

Amongst the headaches facing the GAA are the issue of professionalism and the organisation's amateur status; its ban on members of the British security forces; the recurring calls for Croke Park to be used for soccer internationals; and the perceived threat, from soccer and other sports, to the GAA's ongoing recruitment of new young players.

With Rugby Union having turned professional in the 1990s, further pressure has been placed on the GAA. On a practical level the rugby move could have serious implications for the GAA in the race to attract new players. Will youngsters be lured to rugby at the expense of Gaelic games, drawn by the prospect of financial rewards?

The GAA, at the very least, will need to market its games professionally and treat the youth with absolute respect in the competitive business of player-recruitment. It will need to work harder than ever to attract the very young. Traditionally the GAA was fortunate in that teachers promoted Gaelic games in the schools, even exclusively in the distant past. That has now changed.

Other sports are gaining in popularity, and while Gaelic games have not yet suffered, they will need to be promoted and their players nurtured with enthusiasm and energy. The GAA will also need to develop ladies' football and camogie further.

Vital to the future development of its games and a rise in the standards of play will be more advanced and widespread coaching, with an emphasis on schools and on weaker counties. The Association should continue to play an important role in the social and cultural development of the country, if only for its own sake.

Will the GAA go professional in the twenty-first century? Its instinct would presumably be to say no, but will it have a choice? It may seem unlikely now, but several decades ago the television age would have seemed fanciful and the Internet might have been dismissed as the fantasy of a mad scientist who needed a good night's sleep.

The GAA will in any event have to consider whether or not it intends to pay its players. Perhaps the game will go semi-professional. Most Gaels would be perfectly happy if a compromise of sorts was reached, with players paid good expenses, given perks such as holidays (slowly being introduced at the moment) and encouraged to reap the benefits of sponsorship deals. Players would still essentially be playing for the enjoyment of it, playing too for the pride of club and county. They would still be working and mixing with the 'man in the street'. A desirable compromise, but it may all be too innocent to survive in the future.

The GAA will come under increasing pressure as regards professionalism. Sky TV has spent millions of pounds securing the rights to exclusive coverage of an increasing number of sports worldwide. The Irish national broadcasting station, RTÉ, has covered the games well, and in recent years Ulster Television and the BBC have greatly increased their coverage. None of them, however, can compete financially with Sky.

When Sky does turn its attentions to the GAA, the money on offer may prove irresistible. Sky will be able to tempt the Association with comprehensive coverage of its games, and perhaps also a worldwide audience. In return, Sky would be ensuring that many more Irish homes would pay to join them. If the GAA signs up, who is to say where the journey will take them?

A Super League featuring a given number of top GAA

teams could follow, with players being paid, and sponsorship deals rampant. A transfer system might evolve, with stars moving from one county team to another. Sad thoughts for many GAA fans – but money and time have little regard for sentiment.

There will also be mounting pressure to revoke Rule 21 of the GAA's constitution. The Ban is making no positive contribution to the tense political climate in Northern Ireland; it merely deepens divisions. However, while most politicians and other commentators decry Rule 21 and continue to call for its abolition, the reality is that the GAA rank-and-file supported its retention a few years ago. If there were a political settlement in the North, Rule 21 would surely follow the 'foreign games' ban and find itself consigned to history.

Such a development would create the breathing space in which the GAA and the Protestant community might develop closer ties. In the GAA's early years there were quite a lot of Protestants in the Association, including Douglas Hyde, Ireland's first President. In the North especially they began to drift away once the GAA's nationalist credentials became clear. The irony is that even now some Protestants in the North enjoy watching Gaelic games but continue to feel unwelcome among GAA members.

If the Troubles continue, the GAA will be faced with a stark choice: make a magnanimous decision to revoke Rule 21 – a brave gesture, particularly among those who feel most strongly about the treatment of GAA members by the British security forces; or leave the Ban in place, despite the continued hostility of critics who deem such a stance unworthy of any sporting body.

There have always been soccer fanatics in Ireland. Although Ireland does not have a particularly strong domestic soccer league, the country has frequently produced richly talented players, almost all of whom are quickly lured to Britain once their potential is recognised. In recent years the game's popularity has grown immeasurably throughout the country. One reason is the success of the Irish soccer team, who defied the odds by qualifying for two successive World Cups in the 1990s, almost succeeding at the same time in bringing a delirious country to a standstill. A second reason is the enormous television coverage afforded the game, especially since Sky TV began to monopolise the market.

The growth in the popularity of soccer has manifested itself in the establishment of hundreds of junior soccer clubs and a big rise in the number of children playing the game at school. The general view is that the GAA has succeeded spectacularly in shaking off the threat of soccer, the argument being that it will never be more popular than it was directly after the 1990 and 1994 World Cups – but complacency could prove disastrous. True, attendances at big GAA matches have not dropped, and TV audiences can't get enough of Gaelic games; but it is the children of today who will determine whether or not the GAA will be adversely affected by the soccer surge. Those children are currently showing devotion to top English soccer clubs, wearing their merchandise and singing the praises of their stars.

Of course many children will play both Gaelic and soccer, in which case the GAA must concentrate on making its games more attractive. The continued development of facilities, astute marketing and an improvement in the standard of Gaelic football will all help towards that end.

Should Croke Park open its gates to soccer? Ireland has no national soccer stadium (football's governing body, the FAI, rents the national rugby stadium) and for many years it has been argued that Croke Park should be used as a national stadium, accommodating all sports.

The GAA's historic antipathy towards soccer – the dreaded foreign game – has made this debate all the more heated. To a majority of GAA members, it's not a debate at all. Why should we open our stadium to soccer, they argue. We built it, they're our games; we're *competing* with soccer. A very fair argument.

However, the issue will not go away. When in 1997 the Irish government gave the GAA £20 million towards the ongoing development of Croke Park it was widely rumoured that the grant was on condition that the Association would agree to host soccer internationals in the future. Time will tell.

The need to improve its games, especially Gaelic football, is also on the GAA's agenda. Football, when played in the right spirit, remains a wonderful game. However, there is justified concern at the moment about an increase in the use of spoiling tactics by players. An unwelcome nastiness has crept into the game.

Gaelic football is continually under review, with the GAA conscious of the need to reduce the number of stoppages and instances of violent play and make the game more free-flowing and ultimately more attractive. The two are, of course, linked. The game produces aggression and occasional violence because the win-at-all-costs mentality is encouraged by the absence of a recognised tackle. The exceptional fitness levels attained by players in the 1990s, combined with the running game, mean that opponents are more likely to come into close contact with one another than in the past. This inevitably leads to more bruising exchanges. Referees in turn are under extreme pressure as the game becomes more and more physical.

To its credit the Association is trying to improve the situation, and in 1998 introduced experimental rules in some of its lesser competitions. These include the use of two referees, the introduction of the mark (one of the popular aspects of Australian Rules football) and a clamp-down on rugged tackling. Under these rules a player is automatically booked if he pushes, pulls or holds an opponent. The solo run has also been changed in the hope that it will speed up the game. Improved coaching of referees will be undertaken by the GAA in the coming years.

An essential task for the Association is to try and develop hurling in more counties. The game may be going through a golden era – there are classic games every year, with thrilling hurling and wonderful championship battles – yet while some counties have emerged to challenge the traditional leaders, in many more the game has no credibility, being played only to a low standard or hardly played at all.

At a time when hurling has a high television profile and when fans anticipate each All-Ireland championship with the enthusiasm of children, the GAA should be working to reap the benefits – and spread the game to all parts of Ireland.

A few years ago when a county reached their first All-Ireland football final (which they subsequently won) I was sitting beside an elderly man from that county, a sportswriter by profession, but a GAA man first. I went to shake his hand when his side had won; he was weeping like a child. Recently a man told me that if Roscommon, our county, lost in this year's championship, although a season's hope would be lost, the jersey, its distinctive colour and its meaning would remain. 'They cannot take the jersey away.' As long as such men and such attitudes remain, the GAA will flourish.

The crucial question is: how will the GAA respond to the

changes of today and the challenges of the new millennium? Will the games and the Association be forced to change dramatically? Or will this remarkable organisation with its unique games and its enormous influence on the lives of its members and fans continue the balancing act of being conservative and insular but also immensely popular and the envy of other sports?

Whatever the GAA's woes and its joys, its celebrations and its controversies, the summers will always come. In rural Ireland, the GAA's sacred soil, the turf will be cut and the hay saved. The spirit of the fans will be stirred as time drifts by and the day of the championship game approaches. The hurleys will be stacked against the wall of the dressing-room as the men, togging out, jostle with demons and gods in their minds, wondering what the seventy minutes will bring them. They wouldn't miss it, of course; nor would the footballers: the magic of the games, the nakedness of the beautifully poetic war that is football or hurling. Deep down, the players and the fans all know that this will be their year. This year is always their year, because last year usually wasn't.

With Gaelic games, the summer always comes.